THE MESSAGE OF MERCY

Amalee Meehan is a member of CEIST (Catholic Education An Irish Schools Trust) where she works in the area of faith leadership and governance. She has co-authored two religious education textbooks for US Catholic high schools as part of the *Credo* series. Amalee teaches on the MA in Christian Leadership in Education, Mary Immaculate College, University of Limerick. Her most recent publication is *Joining the Dots: A Programme of Spiritual Reflection and Renewal for Educators* (Veritas).

The Message of Mercy

Amalee
Meehan

VERITAS

Published 2015 by Veritas Publications
7–8 Lower Abbey Street
Dublin 1, Ireland
publications@veritas.ie
www.veritas.ie

ISBN 978 1 84730 652 4

10 9 8 7 6 5 4 3 2 1

Extract from Sebastian Barry's *The Steward of Christendom*
used with kind permission of Bloomsbury Methuen Drama.

A catalogue record for this book is available from the British
Library.

Cover designed by Heather Costello, Veritas Publications
Printed in the Republic of Ireland by SPRINT-print Ltd, Dublin

*Veritas books are printed on paper made from the wood
pulp of managed forests. For every tree felled, at least one
tree is planted, thereby renewing natural resources.*

To Daniel
Fear an Chroí Mhóir

Contents

Acknowledgements

To Donna Doherty and the team in Veritas for your unfailing belief and encouragement. You asked for a book about mercy that could relate to the messiness of life. I hope I have given you something that will resonate with life in its 'ordinary plenty'.

To the Board of Directors of CEIST (Catholic Education an Irish Schools Trust) for granting me leave of absence to write, and to my colleagues in CEIST for the cards, candles and words of good cheer, and for covering for me while I was absent.

To my team of readers – Gerard Meehan, Marion Meehan, Alice Turley and Roger Owens. From the differing perspectives of your busy lives and careers you brought a range of invaluable insights.

To Silvia Tortajada who provided the *cafe con aroma de vainilla*, and brought me into the linguistic world of *misericordiae* and of *Papa Francisco*.

To Sighle whose support in so many ways, not least her generosity and perceptive editing, made this project possible.

To my boys, and especially to Dan – who made it happen, and made it fun.

Míle buíochas,

Amalee

Introduction

Ironman is going to summer camp. He is four-years-old. Baymax, his best friend is going with him. According to camp rules, they are allowed €1 each for the tuck shop. For the first time in their lives, the boys will have their own money to spend as they wish. He can't sleep with the excitement. On the first day, Ironman discovers he has lost his money. He is devastated. They search around, but it is nowhere to be found. Baymax goes to the tuck shop alone. He returns with two giant jelly snakes. He gives one to Ironman. They sit, side by side, and devour their snakes in silence.

That evening, I text Baymax's mum. She replies: 'Baymax loves Ironman. Ironman loves him back. Worth more than € can buy.'

Mercy, from the Hebrew concept of *chesed*, faithfulness between individuals that results in human kindness.[1]

A friend Skypes from the US where she is grading papers. She appears to be at her wit's end. Her Religious Education students haven't done so well in their end of year assessment. She puts some of their answers up on screen (with the bad spelling left in):

‣ The first commandment was when Eve told Adam to eat the apple.
‣ The seventh commandment is, 'Thou shalt not admit adultery'.
‣ The greatest miracle in the Bible is when Joshua told his son to stand still and he obeyed him.
‣ Jesus enunciated the Golden Rule, which says do one to others before they do one to you.

- It was a miracle when Jesus rose from the dead and managed to get the tombstone off the entrance.
- The epistles were the wives of the apostles.
- One of the opossums was St. Matthew who was also a taximan.
- St. Paul cavorted to Christianity. He preached the holy acrimony, which is another name for marriage.
- A Christian should have only one spouse. This is called monotony.

'They know nothing. I've taught them nothing. I should never have become a teacher. I feel like a fraud.' She vents on for a while. 'But they're a great bunch – great kids. We've had some really good conversations. I've enjoyed every moment with them. Maybe next year I'll take a different approach, set a different assignment – one that explores what God means to them, one that connects us more as a group, maybe something where we can engage in an outreach programme with the community or the environment.'

Mercy – sensibility of heart for those in need.[2]

The Absence of Mercy

Having seen so many entertaining adaptations of *Oliver Twist* on stage and screen, the brutality of the novel takes my breath away. Fagin, the corrupt father figure, is an old hand at manipulating childhood innocence for personal gain:

From this day, Oliver was seldom left alone; but was placed in almost constant communication with the two boys, who played the old game with the Jew every day: whether for their own improvement or Oliver's, Mr. Fagin best knew. At other times the old man would tell them stories of robberies he had committed in his younger days: mixed up with so much that was droll and curious, that Oliver could not help laughing heartily, and showing that he was amused in spite of all his better feelings.

In short, the wily old Jew had the boy in his toils. Having prepared his mind, by solitude and gloom, to prefer any society to the companionship of his own sad thoughts in such a dreary place, he was now slowly instilling into his soul the poison which he hoped would blacken it, and change its hue for ever.[3]

The absence of mercy: it defies definition.

The Quality of Mercy

Many English literature scholars and Shakespeare fans will already know that mercy is God's own attribute. Shakespeare presents mercy as a divine quality, worthy of great esteem, valuable in particular to the most powerful people in society.

One of the great speeches in Shakespeare in this regard occurs in *The Merchant of Venice*. Disguised as a young lawyer, Portia has come to rescue Antonio, the merchant of Venice. Antonio foolishly signed a bond granting the usurer Shylock a 'pound of flesh' if he defaults on the loan he was forced to seek. Antonio cannot repay the loan. When Shylock demands to know why he 'must' be merciful, Portia replies that compulsion is precisely contrary to the spirit of mercy. Only because mercy is voluntary – because it mitigates the compulsions of the literal law – is it true mercy. Gentle like heaven's rain, it is a natural and gracious quality rather than a legal one.

> *Portia*:
> The quality of mercy is not strain'd,
> It droppeth as the gentle rain from heaven
> Upon the place beneath: it is twice blest;
> It blesseth him that gives and him that takes:
> 'Tis mightiest in the mightiest: it becomes
> The throned monarch better than his crown;
> His sceptre shows the force of temporal power,
> The attribute to awe and majesty,
> Wherein doth sit the dread and fear of kings;
> But mercy is above this sceptred sway;
> It is enthroned in the hearts of kings,
> *It is an attribute to God himself*;
> And earthly power doth then show likest God's
> When mercy seasons justice ...[4]

According to Portia, no one shows mercy because they have to; it is not something that can be forced. It simply happens, the way gentle rain drops on the ground. Mercy is a double blessing. It blesses the one who gives it and the one who receives it. When it comes from the heart, it is stronger than the strongest power. We ourselves become more like God when human justice mixes with mercy.

Pain and suffering and fractured relationships are universal human experiences, as old as humanity itself.

So too is mercy. 'Patient and merciful' are words which often go together in the Hebrew Scriptures to describe God's nature. Pope Francis describes it as a 'visceral' love. Like that love of a mother or father for their child, it 'gushes forth from the depths naturally, full of tenderness and compassion, indulgence and mercy.'[5] No one can place limits on the love of God.

The Jubilee of Mercy

'Perhaps we have long since forgotten how to show and live the way of mercy,' writes Pope Francis in *Misericordiae Vultus* (The Face of Mercy).[6] This document marks the extraordinary Jubilee of Mercy (the Holy Year of Mercy) which the Pope has called from 8 December 2015 until 20 November 2016, the day celebrated as the feast of Christ the King.

A jubilee year is a special year called by the Church to receive blessing and pardon from God. The Catholic Church has called jubilee years every twenty-five or fifty years since the year 1300 and has also called special (extraordinary) jubilee years from time to time. Explaining his reasons for calling this Jubilee of Mercy, the Pope firmly identifies mercy as the key aspect of Jesus' ministry and the central function of the Church. 'Jesus Christ is the face of the Father's mercy,' he writes. 'Jesus of Nazareth, by his words, his actions, and his entire person reveals the mercy of God.'[7] It is through mercy that Jesus reads the hearts of those he encounters and responds to their deepest need.

Jesus' ministry on earth is a sign of the centrality of mercy in the Christian faith. His person is nothing but love, a love given freely, seeking nothing in return. 'The relationships he forms with the people who approach him manifest something entirely unique and unrepeatable,' states the Pope. 'The signs he works, especially in the face of sinners, the poor, the marginalised, the sick, and the suffering, are all meant to teach mercy. Everything in him speaks of mercy.'

Mercy has been the defining characteristic of the papacy of Pope Francis – a papacy which has resonated deeply with people around the world and touched the hearts of believers and non-believers alike.

Pope Francis

Time magazine's 'person of the year'; Italian *Vanity Fair's* 'man of the year'; 'Person of the Year' in leading gay-rights magazine *The Advocate*; and cover star of *Rolling Stone* – Pope Francis, with his compassionate spirituality and his obvious enjoyment of life, has captured the world's imagination. A former janitor, nightclub bouncer, chemical technician and teacher of literature, his approach is both refreshing and inspiring.

In a matter of months, the new pontiff had placed front and centre the mission of the Church as servant and comforter of people who are hurting in an often harsh world. He has been photographed washing the feet of convicts, posing for selfies with young visitors to the Vatican, embracing a man with a deformed face. He said of women who consider abortion because of poverty or rape, 'Who can remain unmoved before such painful situations?' Of gay people: 'If someone is gay and seeks God and has good will, who am I to judge?'

To divorced and remarried Catholics who are, by rule, forbidden from taking Communion, he says that this crucial rite 'is not a prize for the perfect but a powerful medicine and nourishment for the weak.'[8]

Why Mercy?

What has beguiled us about the papacy of Francis? Walter Kasper, eminent theologian and spiritual director to the pope, says it is his emphasis on mercy. In fact Kasper has written a beautiful book on the topic entitled *Mercy: The Essence of the Gospel and the Key to Christian Life*. But for many people, it is difficult to get a sense of what 'mercy' actually means.

I am used to glazed eyes – particularly my own. I wonder if it is a question of language, because Silvia, my Spanish friend gets it immediately. Silvia does not believe in God and has no truck with any form of organised religion, especially the Catholic Church. And yet she recognises the concept instantly. 'Ah, si – *misericordia* – a deep connection from my heart to yours, especially when you need it most. It will bring a better people, better planet, better humanity.' Even Walter Kasper couldn't say it better![9]

In the first place, it starts with God. Mercy in its truest sense comes from the historical self-revelation of God, who is love (I John 4:8,16). The biblical understanding is of a God who suffers with his creatures, who has a heart (*cor*) with the poor and for the poor (*miseri*), whatever that poverty – material or spiritual – might mean.

In the Bible, the term 'heart' is not understood simply as an internal organ necessary for human life. It describes the core of the human person, the place of his or her deepest feelings and power of judgement. In the Bible, compassion is not regarded as weakness or 'unmanly softness', unworthy of a true hero. Jesus is full of compassion for the widow of Nain who has lost her only son (Luke 77:13). At the death of his friend Lazarus his sadness moves him to tears (John 11:38). The true heroes have merciful hearts that lay claim on their attitudes and actions regarding all their relationships – with family, community, with God and with themselves.

The original words most frequently used to describe merciful attitudes and actions can be rendered as mercy or compassion.[10] These are closely-related terms. Both have a depth of meaning that goes beyond an affective disposition. They denote tenderness and concrete care.

The roots of the English word 'mercy' do not hold the same resonance. Rather than referring to the disposition of a person who exemplifies mercy, it has more to do with the recompense owing to the merciful person. Its roots are in the Latin word 'merces', meaning reward or fee; it is from the same word that the French merci and English terms such as mercantile are derived.

Kasper writes that it is the biblical concept of hesed that comes nearest to a true understanding of God's mercy. The unmerited loving kindness central to hesed goes beyond emotion, sympathy or grief. It means God's free and gracious turning towards the human person, full of care. It concerns a concept of relationship rather than a single action; a disposition or ongoing attitude that disposes the merciful one to action. Applied to God, it is an unmerited and unexpected gift. It exceeds all human expectations and explodes every human category. In the reality of God's *hesed*, something of the mystery of God is revealed.[11]

Inter-Religious Dimension

The practice of mercy is central to both Judaism and Islam. Within the Jewish tradition, the pages of the Hebrew Scriptures are steeped in mercy. The Book of Psalms for instance contains many wonderful verses about mercy, love and hope. Mercy is the term often used in the psalms when talking about God's love and care over us. The truth of God's mercy and love (*ar-Rahman ar-Rahim*) is the central message of Islam. All chapters in the Qur'an, save one, begin with the phrase, 'in the name of God ... the Giver of Mercy.'[12] Indeed, for Pope Francis, interreligious engagement with mercy has the potential to eliminate every form of closed-mindedness and disrespect, and drive out every form of violence and discrimination.

Universal Human Virtues

Kasper describes how compassion and mercy are universal human virtues. As such they can encourage us to engage with other cultures and religions and to work together for understanding and peace in the world. Where compassion and mercy are lost, where egoism and indifference concerning our fellow human beings gain ground, where interpersonal relationship is confined to economic exchanges, the humane nature of society at large is in danger.

But the other side of the story is the countless number of people who give of their time, energy and material means to ease the burden of others. Personal and group commitments contribute to the success of organisations such as the St Vincent de Paul Society, Poverty USA,[13] and Compassion International – a Christian advocacy ministry that helps children out of economic, social, physical and spiritual poverty with the aim of enabling them to become responsible, mature and fulfilled Christian adults.

However, Kasper is concerned with the tendency towards social Darwinism in society today. According to these tendencies, the promotion of one's own selfish interests and the rights of the stronger, without regard for others, are legal tender. Those who are unable to hold their own sink fast. In addition, in the wake of globalisation, unregulated neocapitalist forces have taken hold. For such forces, human beings and entire peoples have become 'collateral damage' in the pursuit of Mammon. In this sphere, it appears that things don't look good for mercy and compassion.

Kasper goes on to say that in order to meet this danger in the West – a danger that cannot be dismissed simply by averting our eyes – Christianity can work with other religions. But first it must plumb the depths of its own tradition of mercy, where the potential is vast. It has shaped Western culture positively and decisively in the past and is urgently needed today.[14] Perhaps that is the strongest motive for this Jubilee of Mercy and the attendant document *Misericordiae Vultus*.

Misericordiae Vultus

In this document, the Pope gives the holy year a motto taken from Luke's Gospel: 'merciful like the father' (Luke 6:36). Mercy is a key quality that indicates God's action towards us. 'The mercy of God is his loving concern for each one of us ... he desires our well-being and he wants to see us happy, full of joy, and peaceful. . . As the Father loves, so do his children. Just as he is merciful, so we are called to be merciful to each other.'[15]

Quoting from Luke's Gospel, Pope Francis reminds us that Jesus asks us, above all, not to judge and not to condemn. 'If anyone wishes to avoid God's judgement, he should not make himself the judge of his brother or sister ... Human beings, whenever they judge, look no farther than the surface, whereas the Father looks into the very depths of the soul.'[16]

Opening Our Hearts

'How many uncertain and painful situations there are in the world today!' writes Pope Francis. 'How many are the wounds borne by the flesh of those who have no voice because their cry is muffled and drowned out by the indifference of the rich,' he continues. 'Let us not fall into humiliating indifference or a monotonous routine that prevents us from discovering what is new!'[17]

The pope advises us to open our hearts 'to those living on the outermost fringes of society: fringes modern society itself creates.' We are compelled to heed their cry for help! 'We cannot escape the Lord's words to us, and they will serve as the criteria upon which we will be judged: whether we have fed the hungry and given drink to the thirsty, welcomed the stranger and clothed the naked, or spent time with the sick and those in prison,' states Pope Francis.[18] His 'burning desire' is that people live the Year of Mercy by engaging with material and spiritual works of mercy.

Mercy and Justice

The first mention of mercy in Luke's Gospel is in the *Magnificat* – Mary's great hymn of praise celebrating the fact that she is to become mother to the Son of God. Despite her initial hesitation and confusion, she recognises God's mercy through his action – the impending incarnation. She knows that it represents the fullness of God's promise to us.

There is a justice element of God's mercy, as Mary communicates it. God scatters those with an arrogant attitude, dethrones rulers who misuse their power and lifts up their victims. Those who have grown wealthy at the expense of the poor are dismissed from the table.

But God's justice is not the justice of the land, of the law, or even of humankind. It is not legal justice, distributive justice (giving each his or her due) or retributive justice (rewarding the good and punishing the bad). Mercy is at the core of God's justice. It stands above the iron fisted logic of guilt and punishment. It is not arbitrary or spontaneous – the product of a momentary whim. At its core is the notion of standing firm.

Pope Francis writes that mercy and justice are not two contradictory realities, but two dimensions of a single reality that unfolds into the fullness of love. The Bible's use of the image of God as a judge, and the frequent depiction of justice as the full observance of the Law and living in conformity with God's commandments, has sometimes led to a legalistic view of justice. But this is a distortion of the original meaning of justice and obscures its profound value.

God's justice includes God's mercy; God's justice is his mercy. Only in this sense can we understand the image of the good and merciful father whom we will meet in the parable in Chapter Two. If God limited himself only to justice, he would cease to be God, and would instead be like human beings who rely on the law. 'But mere justice is not enough,' says Kasper. 'Experience shows that an appeal to justice alone will result in its destruction. This is why God goes beyond justice with his mercy and forgiveness.' Mercy is more than justice or forgiveness although it has those qualities. Justice is cold without mercy. Mercy brings healing, mercy brings joy.

Mercy and Forgiveness

Kasper argues that the concept of mercy, so central to the Bible, has largely been forgotten. It becomes a kind of pseudo-mercy when it is limited to the human idea of justice, or forgiveness, or even empathy. Mercy exceeds all of this. Mercy is larger than justice and larger than forgiveness, because it is the divine birthplace of both. Justice and forgiveness are encompassed in what it means to be merciful.

For Pope Francis, pardoning offences is the clearest expression of merciful love. Pardon is the instrument placed in our hands for the sake of the healing of our own hearts. At times it seems so hard to forgive. To let go of anger, hurt and the desire for revenge are necessary conditions to living joyfully. The pope asks us, as Jesus did, to respond likewise. It is only with merciful hearts that we can read the hearts of others, see them for who they really are, understand them and respond to their deepest needs. This is true of family, friends and colleagues, but also of those on the margins of our society and of world society.

Mercy is God's undeserved, unmerited, often even unsought grace that pours out upon us to help us overcome our miseries and meet our true needs. We see a faint glimpse of it in a parent's love for a child. A child is loved by its parents not because the child has earned or deserved it; rather, the parent's love comes right from the start, a completely free gift, just because the child is the child and the parent is the parent. That depth of human mercy is an image of the divine.

The Gospel of Luke

During the Jubilee, the Sunday readings for Ordinary Time will be taken from Luke's Gospel. Luke is often referred to as 'the evangelist of mercy'. He explains Jesus' message thus: 'be merciful, just as your Father is merciful' (6:36). For Luke, mercy is the essence of God. God looks into our hearts with all their imperfections and draws us out. There is no condemnation, only love. God's mercy is overflowing; it exceeds every human measure. For mercy to be mercy it is unearned, unexpected. It cannot be demanded. We will see this again and again in Luke's gospel, especially in some of the parables exclusive to Luke which have captured the perennial imagination of humankind.

Luke asserts that he carefully researched everything for his entire account. In the opening paragraph he emphasises the reliability of his report (1:2-4). The bookends of Luke's account are Jesus' birth and preparation for ministry on one side, and his passion and Resurrection on the other. In the intervening chapters, Jesus and the disciples undertake a long journey from Galilee to Jerusalem. This entire journey is a dramatic unfolding or revelation of God's kingdom, and how people respond to this unfolding. The 'kingdom of God' denotes what God wills for humankind, a reality of mercy and joy and fulfilment for all people and for the earth itself. A very biblical phrase, it denotes a universal culture of mercy.

Luke's Jesus

It is easy to identify with the Jesus of Luke's Gospel, to be drawn into his world and captured by the effect he has on those who encounter him. He is so incredibly compassionate and courageous. He also gets tired and frustrated. He leans on Simon, but Simon lets him down; he loves his mother, yet he is the sword that breaks her heart. From the early days of his ministry he is surrounded by friends and followers; at the same time there are moments when he clearly, urgently, wants to be on his own.

Luke's Jesus is great company, constantly invited to dinner, even to the homes of his adversaries. Sometimes, he even invites himself! People love to be around him. Table fellowship is central to his ministry. With meals often the fulcrum of his earthly life, on his Resurrection he asks the disciples for something to eat. In Luke's final chapter, fearful and confused disciples are transformed into joyful and confident people of faith after they recognise Jesus in the breaking of the bread.

The humanity of Jesus is real and warm and indisputable. But his core is mercy, God's own attribute. But he is not some sort of therapist, out to assure us that everything is all right and every behaviour acceptable. The Jesus of Luke's Gospel is also challenging. His own people of Nazareth accept him graciously when he returns as a great prophet and leader. That is until he challenges them out of their complacency. When he implies that they need to live into their responsibilities, they become outraged. From this moment, the threat of death hangs in the air.

Luke's Gospel represents a complete reversal of the usually operative human rules. A barren woman like Elizabeth and a virgin like Mary become pregnant (Luke 1:7,34), the powerful are toppled from their thrones and the lowly are lifted up, the hungry are filled with good food while the rich are left empty (Luke 1:52f.). In this way the story is the fulfilment of the Hebrew Scriptures which prophesised all these things. It is spelled out in the Sermon on the Plain (or the Sermon on the Mount in Matthew), according to which and contrary to all human logic, the poor, the mourners, the powerless, the merciful, and the peacemakers are called blessed (Luke 6:20-26, Matthew 5:3-11). It is a history in which God brings about a great levelling. This is a motif.

Jesus preaches more than justice or forgiveness. He preaches dignity and self-worth, freedom and transformation and second chances. He preaches God's own gift to humankind. In short, he preaches mercy. It is to this Jesus we will turn again and again in the chapters that follow – his life, his family, the circle that surrounds him, his conversations and stories. If our task is to open up the mercy of God, there is no better source.

At the heart of Luke's gospel is a teacher who wants each of us to discover again the Golden Rule and what it means for our own lives. We will look at this again in Chapter Three in the context of community. For now, it is enough to outline the three parts at the heart of his message: to really live, to 'have life' we must 'love the Lord your God with all your heart, and with all your soul, and with all your strength, and with all your mind; and your neighbour as yourself … Do this, and you will live' (Luke 10:27-28).

The Law of Love

So there are three aspects to this law of love: love of God; love of neighbour; and love of self. It is these three central relationships that I will examine in the context of mercy. The chapters are structured around these themes. What does it mean to be merciful towards ourselves? How can we be merciful with others? What is it like to be in merciful relationship with God? Whether we are alert to it or not, mercy and the lack of it influences our own lives – our families, the communities we are part of, those unknown to us who can seem very far away, and our relationship with God. From a Christian viewpoint, living joyfully requires the quality of mercy.

Mercy Starts with Our 'Own Selves'

Being able to show mercy towards ourselves, to understand our own souls, is the challenging starting point. *Endless Night* is a lesser-known novel by Agatha Christie, which her niece described as one of her best. In the book, the protagonist is haunted by the notion that he cannot be seen. He has lost so much of his own sense of self he is convinced he is invisible, especially to those he once knew and loved. He is incapable of relationships, incapable of seeing past his own wants and desires. And most frightening of all, he cannot see himself. This is as far from the world that God intends as we can imagine. This is the realm of endless night, the ghost of the fragmented self, ceaselessly roaming in search of integration.

Compare this with the depth of mercy and integration that resonates through *Evangelii Gaudium*. 'I am my mission,' says Pope Francis:

> My mission of being in the heart of the people is not just a part of my life or a badge I can take off; it is not an 'extra' or just another moment in life. Instead, it is something I cannot uproot from my being without destroying my very self. I am a mission on this earth; that is the reason why I am here in this world. We have to regard ourselves as sealed, even branded, by this mission of bringing light, blessing, enlivening, raising up, healing and freeing.[19]

Relationships with those around us – immediate family, friends and colleagues, wider society, and with God – can add to or take from the joy of 'having life.' That is why the dynamic between communal and personal mercy is so important. When we know the sensibilities of our own hearts, it is much more likely that we can engage mercifully with who or what is 'other'.

The Structure of the Book

The five chapters deal with our experiences of mercy and the potential of mercy, each with a different emphasis. They are structured like concentric circles, starting in Chapter One with ourselves in the centre and rippling out through family in Chapter Two and community in Chapter Three. The wider world of which we hear and read, but can avoid encountering unless we decide to, is the subject of Chapter Four. In the final chapter I attempt to say something of our relationship with a merciful God, made even more accessible by the person and promise of Jesus.

Stories, quotes and parables from Luke's Gospel form the framework for each chapter (all biblical references refer to Luke, unless otherwise stated). How mercy plays out in everyday life is the common theme, with examples taken from popular culture, literature, music, and, most especially, shared human experience today. The challenge of human relationships – trying to bring up children well, coping with pressure and loss, doing the best for one's family, participating in local community, engaging with the wider world and building relationship with God – are expressions of the overarching theme. In other words, the qualities of mercy which emerge so beautifully from a close reading of Luke's Gospel continue to resonate with the messiness of life today.

Sources

Numerous sources were helpful to me during this project. Three in particular stayed the course of the journey with me. First is the collective contribution of Pope Francis, from the formal written word and *Misericordiae Vultus* in particular, to his homilies, speeches, interviews and off the cuff remarks; everything about him is an inspiration. Austen Ivereigh's biography *Pope Francis* in particular is an excellent and very enjoyable read.

Second is Walter Kasper's book *Mercy: The Essence of the Gospel and the Key to Christian Life*; the timely publication of this excellent work saved me a considerable amount of heavy lifting. His wealth of knowledge and vibrant style of communication, translated from German with such sympathy by William Madges, contributed greatly to my enjoyment of the process. I found in the works of Charles Dickens an understanding of mercy from the Victorian age, akin to that explained in the twentieth century by Kasper. It comes to life in a particular way in the novel *Oliver Twist*; this too forms a thread through the chapters.

Finally, www.livingspace.ie is a website of the Irish Jesuits offering a comprehensive collection of commentaries on scripture readings. Living Space is part of the prayer site www.sacredspace.ie, also run by the Irish Jesuits. Their insights into Scripture are invaluable; the section on Luke's Gospel is particularly helpful.

A Word about the Superheroes

This book was meant to give a contemporary understanding of the notion of mercy, relevant to the lives of ordinary people. But I made the grave mistake of introducing some superheroes in the first few pages. Having got themselves on paper, they proceeded to pop up at regular intervals. It is only with the greatest difficulty that I managed to retain any pages to devote to the great figures of Luke's Gospel.

At times these figures seemed to walk the journey with me: John the Baptist who begins Luke's account with great promise and confidence but midway through shows signs of doubt; Peter, the rock, who strides through every chapter until his miserable failure when the cock crows. Yet almost immediately, he pulls himself and the little community together, and emerges as a leader that will leave it strong, brave and enduring. And of course Mary, whose love for her son echoes that of every mother; whose agony no one would dare to imagine. All of these in their different ways are expositions of mercy. That is the journey of this book.

CHAPTER ONE

Landscapes of the Heart:
The Inward Experience of Mercy

What I do is me: for that I came.
Gerard Manley Hopkins, 'As Kingfishers Catch Fire'

Lady Mary Crawley of *Downton Abbey* knows exactly who she is. And if she ever forgets, even for a moment, her grandmother the Dowager Countess of Grantham will remind her. Lady Mary is the eldest daughter of the Earl of Grantham as well as the mother of the current heir of Grantham, George. As a member of the early twentieth century British upper class, she knows how to dine, how to dress, how to behave. Her social standing dictates almost every aspect of her life.

And yet, at her core, we glimpse something much more meaningful, something unveiled slowly as she discovers depths in herself through her relationship with Matthew. 'Mine is the true Mary,' he tells her. Matthew helps her to realise a tender compassion and a need for love, hidden even to herself beneath her strong will and sometimes cruel arrogance. In allowing herself to love Matthew she uncovers, to her own surprise, a sensibility of heart.

Mercy: sensibility of heart for those in need (even if that need is our own).

A Denial of Mercy

Moving from a contemporary period drama to a classic nineteenth century novel, we see a similar theme but from a completely different perspective. Catherine Earnshaw of *Wuthering Heights*, on the other hand, denies her deepest self with tragic consequences. In the novel *Wuthering Heights* we witness the terrible fallout that ensues when we deny mercy to ourselves. Catherine marries Edgar Linton although Heathcliff is the man she truly loves. But she cannot admit to that love; she cannot be faithful to her own heart. A pivotal moment comes when Heathcliff appears in the Linton home of Thrushcross Grange after a long period of absence. Lifting the dying Cathy into his arms, he drops to his knees and asks 'why did you betray your own self?' Cathy is clearly dying, of a broken heart and a broken spirit. Cutting off Heathcliff to marry Linton is so destructive that she destroys not only something of her own self but also of Heathcliff – the only person she ever loved. After death, her spirit is left to haunt the moors, searching for what she has lost.

If mercy is faithfulness that results in human kindness, Catherine's denial speaks only of its absence.

In *Wuthering Heights* Emily Brontë captures something of the human quest to know oneself (identity) and remain true (faithful) to that self. At the heart of the human condition is a search for completeness – to become our 'own selves'. It is an insight as old as the Scriptures, true for instance of the Prodigal Son. Luke tells us that when the younger son has hit rock bottom, alone in a foreign land, he 'comes to himself' (15:17). In that dawning realisation the younger son understands who he really is, where he is from, and yearns to go back.

'Coming to Ourselves'

'Coming to ourselves' is as central to the human search for completeness as it ever was. Indeed, the fragmented self is a well-documented phenomenon today, typified by increasing loneliness among young people and an ongoing spiritual hunger prevalent in Western culture. Identity and rootedness, or more accurately, lack of both – personal and communal – is at the heart of this fragmentation. Only by attending to the sensibility of heart through addressing questions such as who we are, who or what is 'the other' and what our purpose in life might be, can integration take place.

Rootlessness and Loneliness

Our postmodern culture is characterised by a rootlessness showing itself in a diminished sense of the past and distrust of tradition, a kind of cultural amnesia, a lostness and loneliness. With no sense of who we are or where we came from, a new isolation takes hold.

For instance, in 2010 the UK Mental Health Foundation found loneliness to be a greater concern among young people than the elderly. The eighteen to thirty-four-year-olds surveyed were more likely to feel lonely, to worry about feeling alone and to feel depressed because of loneliness than the over-fifty-fives. Loneliness is inextricably linked with mental health issues such as stress, depression, paranoia, anxiety, addiction, cognitive decline and can be a significant factor in suicide.

Doctor Grant Blank, a survey research fellow at the Oxford Internet Institute, points out that social media and the internet can be a boon and a problem. They are beneficial when they enable us to communicate with distant loved ones, but not when they replace face-to-face contact. People present an idealised version of themselves and their social lives online. We expect to have social lives like those portrayed in the media; we feel the need to present numerous social engagements and countless 'friends' online, whether that is a true representation or not. Comparing friends' seemingly perfect lives with our own can lead us to withdraw socially. Indeed, a 2013 study of social media at the University of Michigan found that Facebook reduces life satisfaction.[21]

For Ruth Sutherland, the chief executive of UK relationship counselling organisation Relate, the antidote to reducing our isolation rests on laying the foundations to good-quality relationships earlier in life. But good quality interpersonal relationships depend on empathy, compassion and kindness.[22] In other words, healthy relationships depend exactly on the qualities that characterise the mercy of Jesus of Nazareth.

But merciful relationships with others are contingent on a merciful relationship with oneself. This implies a need for a kind of 'inward mercy' – a self–awareness and the ability to be faithful to that self. We cannot give what we don't have. Merciful relationships require a merciful heart, and that starts with the ability to be merciful towards oneself.

The Gift of Inward Mercy

Jean Valjean is another great character who struggles with issues of self-awareness and awareness of others.

What separates his redemption from the ceaseless roaming of Catherine Earnshaw is his mercy towards himself, what we have termed 'inward mercy.' The hero of Victor Hugo's epic *Les Misérables*, Valjean is condemned as a criminal and hunted as an escaped convict. When another man is arrested in his place in a case of mistaken identity, Valjean has the chance to flee his past forever. But he can't do it. He cannot pretend he doesn't see the other; he cannot ignore the awful fate that awaits him.

In the musical adaptation of the novel, this struggle reaches breaking point just before the trial of the arrested man. Valjean knows that to ignore the 'innocent who bears his face' is to compromise his name, his identity, his own self. If he conceals himself now, at the very moment when mercy is most needed, he will never again be able to face either himself or his fellow human beings. He asks 'Who am I?' and declares to himself and to the court: 'I'm Jean Valjean'.

The ability of Valjean to look deep into his own soul and meet what he finds there; his ability to see and be moved by the plight of the wrongfully accused man is a beautiful example of mercy at work. It becomes the redemptive force for the wrongfully accused man, for his own soul, and ultimately for his relationship with God. The question that plagues him is a question that we all face, at some point in our lives: 'Who am I?' The question that follows closely on its heels is different but connected: 'What am I doing here?'/'What is my place in this world?' Although different questions, they are clearly linked and are often referred to as issues of identity and purpose.

Identity and Purpose (According to Luke)

Luke casts identity and purpose as two sides of the same coin. This is particularly true in his presentations of John and Jesus. Luke is a meticulous and thoughtful historian. For him, the ministries of John and Jesus did not commence at their first public appearances, but at the time of the announcement of their births. Immediately after the short introduction to his Gospel, Luke begins the intertwined account of the births of two boys – John and Jesus. The birth of John, the forerunner of Christ, is first.

John the Baptist

Luke wants us to be aware that John's purpose in life was formed from factors which took place in his earliest years. And so, unlike the other Gospel writers, Luke introduces the Baptist with the angelic announcement of his birth. To his childless parents, Elizabeth and Zechariah, it is a miracle. Both are elderly, both are descendants of the priestly tribe of Aaron, and both live in accordance with the Law of Moses. There is no apparent reason for their shame, for in the eyes of first-century society it is a source of great shame that they have had no children.

As his forefathers were before him, Zechariah is a priest in the holy sanctuary. One day, while carrying out the privileged task of offering incense in the holy place, the angel Gabriel appears announcing the birth of a child to him and his wife in their old age. Gabriel's news comes with instructions: 'your wife Elizabeth will bear you a son, and you will name him John' (1:13).

The child will be the forerunner of the promised Messiah as prophesised in the Hebrew Scriptures (1:17). Out of doubt, Zechariah asks for a confirming sign; he needs to be convinced before he goes home with the story. But he is rebuked by Gabriel and struck mute (1:20).

Elizabeth does indeed bear the 'miracle child'. Her neighbours and relatives recognise that 'great mercy' (1:58) has been shown to her, and they rejoice with her in this blessing.

The Naming of John

In the culture of the Israelites, a name was not simply a means of identification. It denoted the essence of a person, the 'who am I?' as well as the 'what is my purpose?' So the naming of a child was a very significant event. God sometimes changed the name of a person to reflect a special role or appointment, for instance Abram to Abraham, Sarai to Sarah, and Jacob to Israel. In this case, as with that of Jesus, God gives the name of the child before birth.

But the naming of the baby quickly becomes a divisive and emotional issue, with Elizabeth standing firm against a group of neighbours and relatives. Everyone presumes he will be given the name of his father. To be named by any other name implied a departure from family, lineage and role in society. The neighbours and relatives argue with Elizabeth: 'none of your relatives has this name' (1:61). Without his father's name, the child would not follow in his father's steps. He would not be a priest. He would not learn the priestly ministries of the temple.

Elizabeth's insistence that the boy be named John is to renounce the family, its work, and its perpetuation through the next generation. It is a courageous move for an elderly couple with their miracle baby. Every parent wants the best for their children. By naming him John, Elizabeth and Zechariah accept a very uncertain future for their only child.

The resolution of this standoff comes when Zechariah is consulted using signals and gestures. He writes the words 'his name is John' on a tablet. In that short sentence are all the seeds of the baby's identity and purpose – seeds that will flower in the desert and will not die at the feet of Salome. All of the neighbours and relatives are amazed. 'All these things were talked about throughout the entire hill country of Judea. All who heard them pondered them and said, "What then will this child become?"' (1:65-66).

The Biblical meaning of the name John is 'the grace or mercy of the Lord.' John's role in life will be very different from what was originally expected: he will communicate the sensibility of the heart of God to the people of Israel and prepare them for the coming of Jesus:

> … even before his birth he will be filled with the Holy Spirit. He will turn many of the people of Israel to the Lord their God. With the spirit and power of Elijah he will go before him, to turn the hearts of parents to their children, and the disobedient to the wisdom of the righteous, to make ready a people prepared for the Lord (1:15-17).

John: The Mercy of God

'His name is John.' In that moment of naming the baby, Zechariah once again gains the power of speech: 'Immediately his mouth was opened and his tongue freed, and he began to speak, praising God' (1:64). In the beautiful prayer that follows known as the *Benedictus*, it is Zechariah, the man who was struck mute, who articulates the significance of the event. Zechariah uses the language of mercy, reflecting the essence of his son: 'the God of Israel has ... shown mercy promised to our ancestors' (1:68, 72). Just as the miracle child is a gift of mercy to Zechariah and Elizabeth, so he will be a gift of mercy to the people of Israel:

> And you, child, will be called the prophet of the
>   Most High;
>   for you will go before the Lord to prepare his ways,
> to give knowledge of salvation to his people
>   by the forgiveness of their sins.
> By the tender mercy of our God,
>   the dawn from on high will break upon us,
> to give light to those who sit in darkness and in the
>   shadow of death,
>   to guide our feet into the way of peace (1:76-79).

John remains faithful to his identity and purpose to the point of his untimely death at the hands of Herod. However, it is not always so straightforward, and certainly not so for many people today. Knowing oneself is a journey of self-discovery; remaining faithful to that self often involves considerable courage. But both are essential to the gift of inward-mercy.

The Journey to Inward Mercy

Self-discovery can be frightening, even more so because it is never ending. We never reach complete knowledge of ourselves, just as we can never attain complete knowledge of someone else or of God. This is the ancient insight of Rabbi Zusya. Before he died, Rabbi Zusya said: 'In the world to come they will not ask me, "Why were you not Moses?" They will ask me, "Why were you not Zusya?"' But as we have already seen, those who shy away from self-knowledge and inward mercy, consciously or unconsciously, also have the most trouble understanding life, love and relationships.

Both John and Jesus grow up in loving homes, with strong and supportive parents. But that is not the same for everybody; it is not always the case. The circumstances of our births, the homes we're reared in and our childhood influences have a major part to play in helping or hindering us to discover who we are and our purpose in life. This is a theme common among many great authors, including Charles Dickens. The characters of Nancy and Rose, the two primary female figures in *Oliver Twist*, are both essentially good and noble. But their different paths in life lead them in two dramatically different directions, resulting in the brutal murder of one and enduring happiness for the other.

'Stay another moment,' interposed Rose ... 'Will you return to this gang of robbers, and to this man? ... What fascination is it that can take you back, and make you cling to wickedness and misery?'

'When ladies as young, and good, and beautiful as you are,' replied [Nancy] steadily, 'give away your hearts, love will carry you all lengths … When such as I, who have no certain roof but the coffin-lid, and no friend in sickness or death but the hospital nurse, set our rotten hearts on any man, and let him fill the place that has been a blank through all our wretched lives, who can hope to cure us?'[23]

Nancy represents all the degradation into which poverty and loneliness can force otherwise good people. Rose, on the other hand, embodies all the advantage that comes from loving surroundings. The role of one's environment in distinguishing vice from virtue is clear: the same compassion and loyalty to a loved one that is a virtue in Rose is a self-destructive force for Nancy, binding her to her vice-ridden lover Sikes.

Rose asks Nancy: 'What fascination is it that can take you back, and make you cling to wickedness and misery?' Although utterly inexplicable to Rose, who has only ever been surrounded by people who love and care for her, Nancy's compulsion to return echoes through the lives of very many people today. We can get drawn into situations that we know are not good for us; we find ourselves returning to relationships that are destructive, often for reasons that may not be clear even to ourselves. Acting in a way that is congruent with our deepest selves, our best selves, is not always easy. In fact, it is often very difficult.

Psychotherapists say that poor self-confidence and low self-esteem are perhaps the most influential factors on this type of behaviour. Nancy is compelled to return because she feels she is no better and deserves no better than Sikes. She despises herself for what she has become but can see no way out. Nancy asks for pity, but what she needs is mercy: the mercy of Rose and others in society, and even more so, mercy for herself. Nancy's story illustrates the connection between the ability to make good choices and live life well on the one hand, and to have mercy on oneself on the other.

The Christian tradition proposes that a level of self-awareness and awareness of one's role in life, the ability to know one's heart and its deepest desires, helps us to make good choices and live well. Catherine of Siena says: 'If you are what you should be, you will set the world on fire.' But it is not always easy. Sometimes it is really hard to be oneself. There is all that we don't like, all that we want to leave behind. This is where inward mercy is so important; being merciful with oneself makes the process easier. With inward mercy, self-resistance falls away to allow for the becoming of who we are made to be.

Spiritual Hunger

The human search for completeness and the need for inward mercy is nothing new. But our traditional modes of searching, those that steer us 'outward and upward' as well as inward, have been fractured. Instead of guiding us down the road of mercy, contemporary quests can circle back in on ourselves. The fallout is an acute spiritual hunger tied to a sense of desolation, reflected in the rapidly growing market for self-help manuals and spiritually themed books of many types.

Let's take for example, Oprah's Book Club. When the show concluded in May 2011, Nielsen BookScan created a list of the top-ten bestsellers from the club's final ten years (prior data was unavailable). The top three bestsellers are as follows:

1. Eckhart Tolle, *A New Earth*, 3,370,000 copies
2. James Frey, *A Million Little Pieces*, 2,695,500 copies
3. Elie Wiesel, *Night*, 2,021,000 copies.[24]

It is interesting that in different ways, all of these books point to questions of self-awareness, awareness of others and finding one's purpose in life. Take for instance, the most popular choice: New York Times bestseller Eckhart Tolle's *A New Earth: Awakening to your Life's Purpose*. According to Tolle, the book's purpose 'is not to add new information or beliefs to your mind or to try to convince you of anything, but to bring about a shift in consciousness.'[25] He envisions a world population that is increasingly more humble, enlightened and pure and that involves a massive change in group think. The book encourages its readers to live their lives in each present moment and to create happiness for themselves without emphasizing material possessions. When Eckhart Tolle partnered Oprah for a series of webinars based on the book, they attracted more than eleven million viewers.

A Million Little Pieces tells the story of a 23-year-old alcoholic and drug abuser and his rehabilitation in a twelve steps-oriented treatment centre. (When it became clear that James Frey had fabricated large parts of his 'memoir', Oprah was forced to abandon her initial defence of the author and apologise to her viewers).

Night is the first book in a trilogy – *Night, Dawn, Day* – reflecting author Eli Wiesel's state of mind during and after the Holocaust. The titles mark Wiesel's own journey from darkness to light, reflecting the Jewish tradition of beginning a new day at nightfall. In *Night*, he said, 'I wanted to show the end, the finality of the event. Everything came to an end – man, history, literature, religion, God. There was nothing left. And yet we begin again with night.'[26]

Pope Francis is acutely in tune with this spiritual hunger and how we are tempted to feed it: 'The great danger in today's world, pervaded as it is by consumerism, is the desolation and anguish born of a complacent yet covetous heart, the feverish pursuit of frivolous pleasures, and a blunted conscience.'[27] For Francis, the joy of the Gospel, the mercy of the kingdom as preached and lived by Jesus, is a sure way to consolation, contentment and real fulfilment. This is the route to filling the blank in all our lives.

Jesus and the Mercy of the Kingdom

Just as with the naming of John, Jesus' purpose is tied up with his identity from the very beginning. The angel Gabriel is unequivocal with Mary. The child's name will be Jesus (God with us). The infant will be the Son of God. He will be called 'the Son of the Most High' and … 'will reign over the house of Jacob forever. Of his kingdom there will be no end' (1:32-33). Despite this, his parents are amazed at the reaction of Simeon, the wise old man of the temple who looks right into the heart of the infant and delights in what he sees:

Simeon took him in his arms and praised God, saying,

'Master, now you are dismissing your servant in
    peace,
    according to your word;
for my eyes have seen your salvation,
    which you have prepared in the presence of all
    peoples,
a light for revelation to the Gentiles
    and for glory to your people Israel.'

And the child's father and mother were amazed at
what was being said about him (2:28-33).

The Baptism of Jesus is a pivotal moment in his journey
to fullness. If there had been any doubts about his
identity they are summarily dispatched by the voice
from the heavens: 'you are my Son, the Beloved; with
you I am well pleased' (3:22). By the time his temptation
in the desert is complete, Jesus is a fully mature adult,
clear about who he is and his purpose on earth. He sets
out his stall with great clarity on the occasion of his first
public engagement. For that, he goes back to his home
town of Nazareth:

When he came to Nazareth, where he had been
brought up, he went to the synagogue on the
sabbath day, as was his custom. He stood up to read,
and the scroll of the prophet Isaiah was given to him.
He unrolled the scroll and found the place where it
was written:
    'The Spirit of the Lord is upon me,
    because he has anointed me
    to bring good news to the poor.

He has sent me to proclaim release to the captives
and recovery of sight to the blind,
to let the oppressed go free,
to proclaim the year of the Lord's favour.'

And he rolled up the scroll, gave it back to the
attendant, and sat down. The eyes of all in the
synagogue were fixed on him. Then he began to say
to them, 'Today this scripture has been fulfilled in
your hearing' (4:16-21).

The Ministry of Jesus

The opening words of Jesus' sermon recall his Baptism:
the Spirit of the Lord has anointed him for a purpose.
The ministry of Jesus brings about pardon of prisoners,
recovery of sight to the blind, the burdened and
battered set free. His concern is for those who suffer the
crushing effects of poverty – economic, physical and
spiritual. His good news extends to those who are grief
stricken, poor with suffering, trapped in destructive
situations and blind to the possible ways out.

But there is a challenge to his words – that is the
vexing character of his message. Once he has the full
attention of his Nazarene audience he tells them 'today
this scripture has been fulfilled in your hearing' (4:21). If
this is said to you, in your hearing, then you have a part
to play. God expects us to do what is right and just and
kind. God expects us to be merciful.

The year of the Lord's favour that Jesus proclaims
here is analogous to Pope Francis' Year of Mercy. Jesus'
purpose as he announces it to the people of Nazareth

resonates with the purpose of the Jubilee of Mercy: 'to bring a word and gesture of consolation to the poor, to proclaim liberty to those bound by new forms of slavery in modern society, to restore sight to those who can see no more because they are caught up in themselves, to restore dignity to all those from whom it has been robbed.'[28]

Living the Message of Mercy

Jesus not only proclaims the message of God's mercy, he lives it himself. He sees into the hearts of those he meets and is moved by compassion to help them. The episodes immediately after the scene in Nazareth show Jesus beginning to practise what he preaches. He frees a man from demons (4:31–37), heals Simon's mother-in-law (4:38–39), and reaches out to touch, heal, and free everyone who comes to him for help (4:40–41). The rest of the Gospel of Luke tells of Jesus healing and welcoming even the most crushed and downtrodden people: social outcasts, broken-hearted parents, prostitutes, the beggars and the homeless.

He forgives them and frees them, welcomes them and changes them. His purpose is a new community that breaks down the barriers between insider and outsider, Jew and Gentile, rich and poor, slave and free. Even on the cross he pardons the repentant thief and prays for those who had brought him to that violent end (23:34-43). Here is a glimmer of the kingdom of God – the universal culture of mercy. Jesus' invitation to each one of us to do our bit in bringing it about is as relevant as ever in the world of today. For Christians, Jesus' purpose is the model of Christian purpose – it is the model of living that will bring us closest to God and closest to ourselves.

The Help of Others

Whether we like it or not, those closest to us have a role in helping us to discern our identity and purpose. We need others in our journey to inward mercy. How others see us, how they relate to us, tells us something about ourselves, our gifts, our strengths and vulnerabilities. They can help us towards a sensibility of heart.

Mary and Elizabeth

The story of Mary and her cousin Elizabeth is perhaps one of the great stories of confirmation of identity and purpose in the Bible. Two pregnant women meet and rejoice in their good news.

After the Angel Gabriel left her, 'Mary set out and went with haste to a Judean town in the hill country' (1:39). She knows, because Gabriel has told her, that Elizabeth too has good news – great news. Married to Zechariah for many years, Elizabeth has waited for a baby in vain. Now, in her old age, she is in her sixth month 'for her who was said to be barren' (1:36).

Mary enters the house of Zechariah and greets Elizabeth. Her cousin immediately recognises that Mary has been blessed in an extraordinary way and that the child in her womb, only a tiny thing, is also blessed. She utters the famous words from the Hail Mary: 'Blessed art thou among women, and blessed is the fruit of thy womb Jesus' (1:41). Elizabeth is the first to understand the unique role of Mary. She knows by the way her own unborn child leaped in her womb. Elizabeth is humbled, asking: 'And why is this granted to me, that the mother of my Lord comes to me? (1:43) Her reaction of confirmation and celebration offers reassurance to her young cousin for the road ahead.

Or course it does not always work like that; the reverse is also true. The most serious upsets to our ideas of ourselves and how we relate to life can come from those closest to us. And sometimes friends and family have trouble recognising us for who we are or supporting what we consider to be our purpose. The greatest challenges can come from inside. There is a passage in Luke's Gospel where we see something similar. The first real questioning of Jesus and his mission comes from a most unlikely quarter.

John's Moment of Doubt

We have already seen something of the relationship between John the Baptist and Jesus. A close reading of the four gospels suggests that John is the firmest ally to Jesus. Of the same age, of the same family, probably childhood friends, John goes ahead to prepare the way. Yet it is from that relationship that a public challenge to Jesus arises. The friendship between John the Baptist and Jesus is a favourite theme of artists over the centuries. So how do we explain the episode where John seems to question Jesus – not his approach, not even his ministry, but his very identity?

Luke tells us that the disciples of John reported to him news of what Jesus had been up to: 'Jesus had just then cured many people of diseases, plagues, and evil spirits, and had given sight to many who were blind' (7:21). So John summoned two of his disciples and sent them to the Lord to ask, 'Are you the one who is to come, or are we to wait for another?' (7:19). They repeat his question exactly: 'John the Baptist has sent us to you to ask, "Are you the one who is to come, or are we to wait for another?"' (7:20). It seems as though John is publicly questioning if Jesus really is the Messiah.

Why John's Unease?

It is important to note that Luke offers no explanation for John's question to Jesus. Perhaps he was simply growing impatient. John had been preaching about a radical leader, one who would effect significant change. But rather than bringing about a dramatic overthrow, Jesus seems to be wandering through the countryside with a group of friends. Either way, it seems as though John is trying to help things along. Jesus needs to proclaim himself as Messiah or his disciples will turn to another. But this is not the way of Jesus. Jesus did not want people to accept him as the Messiah because he claimed to be the Messiah, but because the evidence was irrefutable.

In many ways Jesus' response to this encounter is one of the most lovely examples of mercy in Luke's Gospel because it mirrors a very human situation. It is often those closest to us that cause and take most offence by misunderstanding what we are trying to do. But Jesus refuses to go down that route. He knows the heart of John, knows who he is at his core, and directs his response to the very essence of the man. He does not pander, humiliate, intimidate or point score; he does not jump to John's demands, smother him with personal attention or tell John the answers to his problems, which might have put his mind at ease.

His response is very simple. He simply tells John's emissaries to explain to the Baptist what they had witnessed: 'Go and tell John what you have seen and heard: the blind receive their sight, the lame walk, the lepers are cleansed, the deaf hear, the dead are raised, the poor have good news brought to them' (7:22).

And that is a perfectly clear and unambiguous answer to their question. All the Jewish community including John would have been familiar with the long awaited Messianic prophecy of Isaiah which Jesus read to the community at Nazareth: 'the Spirit of the Lord brings good news to the poor, proclaims release to the captives and recovery of sight to the blind' (4:18-19).

The signs of the coming of the long-awaited Messiah, are clearly being realised in Jesus. He could not have given a stronger indication of his identity. The answer then is clearly: 'Yes. Jesus is the one who is to come because all these things are happening before your very eyes.'

The signs of the Messiah's presence are strange indeed. It is not a manifestation of political power or the destruction of traditional enemies nor is it found in a complex set of doctrinal beliefs. The Messiah's presence brings about physical and spiritual healing, the restoring of people to wholeness in their individual and social lives and in their relationship with God – in short, a universal culture of mercy.

Take No Offence

Jesus' final message to John is one of encouragement: 'blessed is anyone who takes no offence at me' (7:23). Take no offence, John. All the reassurance you need is right here. Trust in God, in your relationship with God. Try not to get side-tracked or despondent. Remain faithful to yourself and to your role in all of this.

But Jesus appreciates the cost to John the Baptist: 'I tell you, no one born of women is greater than John; yet the least in the kingdom of God is greater than he' (7:28). In Jesus, humanity glimpses 'earth as it is in heaven'. This was a privilege that John was never to know. John is the messenger, the one who goes before. He doesn't live to see the effect of Jesus. The closest John gets to the ministry of Jesus is the reports from his messengers.

The Role of the Wider Community

In Luke's telling, the identity of Jesus is frontloaded; Mary is told by means of an angelic announcement in the first chapter that Jesus is the 'Son of God' (1:35). But wider recognition takes time. Even the community he gathers around him has to warm to the knowledge.

Initially it is adversaries rather than followers of Jesus who recognise him. 'I know who you are,' says the unclean demon (4:34); the evil spirits who plague the sick shout, 'You are the Son of God!' (4:41).

Those who support and follow Jesus are slower off the mark. For Peter and the disciples, it takes quite a while for the penny to drop. Even after Jesus calms the storm they ask, 'Who then is this, that he commands even the winds and the water, and they obey him?'

(8:25). When Herod asks the same question it strikes an ominous note: 'John I beheaded; but who is this about whom I hear such things?' (9:7-9).

Then, quite suddenly, just before their departure for the long journey from Galilee to Jerusalem, Jesus confirms his identity. What starts with Jesus asking in a general way, 'Who do the crowds say that I am?' ends with a direct question, 'but who do you say that I am?' It is followed by an equally direct answer. Peter responds, 'The Messiah of God,' a statement which Jesus confirms (9:18-20).

Once his identity has been established among the disciples, Jesus and the group start out on the long road to Jerusalem. There the crowds throw their cloaks on the path as he approaches and shout loudly 'blessed is the king'. All efforts towards discretion are futile. Crowds have gathered to celebrate the Messiah; even if they were silent, 'the stones would shout out' (9: 36-40). But it is a transitory acknowledgement. The same crowd that exalts his entry into Jerusalem will rabidly insist on his crucifixion.

Full, real and true recognition comes with the Resurrection. The disciples on the road to Emmaus recognise him in the breaking of the bread: 'then their eyes were opened and they recognised him' (24:31). They return to Jerusalem to find that others have reached the same depth of understanding: 'The Lord has risen indeed' (24:34).

Conclusion

Mercy, so important to human well-being, begins at home. Inward mercy, or the ability to look deeply into ourselves and deal honestly and compassionately with what we find there, is the starting point because it points us towards identity and purpose.

Coming to terms with one's identity and purpose is not reliant on self-promotion or public proclamations. It cannot happen by amassing 'friends' on social network sites, the 'feverish pursuit of frivolous pleasures' or running madly through life. It involves a journey of self-discovery and inward mercy. May Sarton expresses something of this when she writes:

> Now I become myself. It's taken
> Time, many years and places;
> I have been dissolved and shaken,
> Worn other people's faces …[29]

We have seen how important this journey is in a world characterised by lostness, loneliness and spiritual hunger. But it is not one we can take solely by ourselves; we need the help of others. Inward mercy cannot be separated from merciful relationship with others.

The back and forth of time immersed in family and community is very significant in shaping who we are and how we live. Family is so important to Luke that he spends almost his entire first chapter outlining the lineage of Jesus. The influence of the family environment is impossible to ignore. It is to family, specifically the mercy of fathers and mothers, that we now turn.

CHAPTER TWO

Parents and Children:
A Deep Well of Mercy

I am rich in children, but they are driving me stark raving muttering insane.

I think there are three of them, but they sprint through the house and scream piercingly and slam doors … The children call me name and use bad words and hide clothes under their beds and take their mother for granted and get sick all the time and cough darkly on me and put their muddy feet on the couch … They have broken two windows and cracked a door … They lose their homework, their hats, their jackets, their backpack, their tempers.

Yet when they are sick they drape themselves on me like warm shirts, which I love, and they leave me notes sometimes in my shoes, which I love … and when they hug me they hug me desperately and powerfully, and they murmur like small owls when they are sleepy, and they are hilarious twice a day and sometimes, not very often, not as often as I would like, they turn to me and cup my grizzled face in their grubby hands and do the Vulcan mind-lock thing, their sea-green eyes drilling into me, and that is when I am most sure that I am a man wealthy beyond words in the only coin that matters, love, harried though it may be.[30]

Being a parent is a source of great joy. But the parenting learning curve is steep, unpredictable, full of challenges and surprises. The perfect child does not exist, nor does the perfect parent. There is no foolproof guide or impeccable manual on parenting. Luke's Gospel is very real in this regard. It is full of family gatherings, family disputes, family emergencies and celebrations. He deals with mothers, fathers, sisters, cousins, and lots of sets of brothers. Family dynamics, as complex in first century Palestine as they are today, run throughout his account. In this chapter I focus on the theme of mothers and fathers in merciful relationship with their children, because Luke's treatment of both says so much about the quality of mercy.

Fathers, Stepfathers, Father Figures

Many people will recognise the parable of the Prodigal Son as one of the most memorable illustrations of a merciful parent, not only in Luke's Gospel but in all of Scripture. Before we move in that direction however, it is worth noting that the importance of parental mercy can also be explained by its absence.

In the novel *Oliver Twist*, Fagin appears to be the benign, charity-dispensing father figure, aiding street-boys who have no homes, while in fact he trains and runs them as a pack of thieves. Dickens presents Fagin as the evil and merciless stepfather, the opposite of the good and merciful father, Mr Brownlow. Fagin is repulsive, dirty, wily and duplicitous, a child kidnapper and treasure hoarder. Often times he is like the Prince of Darkness himself, a 'loathsome reptile' with claws and fangs; other times as a 'merry old gentleman' cunning and charming enough to retain his power over the criminal network, especially Nancy and the boys.

Dickens introduces Fagin to Oliver and to the reader by painting an obviously Satanic portrait. When the Artful Dodger throws open the door of the thieves' blackened kitchen, there stands Fagin – a red-haired devil, standing over the fire, with a pitchfork in his hand:

> ... whose villainous-looking and repulsive face was obscured by a quantity of matted red hair. He was dressed in a greasy flannel gown ... Seated round the table were four or five boys, none older than the Dodger, smoking long clay pipes, and drinking spirits with the air of middle-aged men. These all crowded about their associate ... and then turned round and grinned at Oliver. So did the Jew himself, toasting-fork in hand.
>
> 'This is him, Fagin,' said Jack Dawkins; 'my friend Oliver Twist.'[31]

Dickens is crystal clear: without the influence of a merciful parent, there is very little hope for these boys.

The Merciful Father

Then there is a different type of father – the type whose love knows no ends. The Jesus of Luke's Gospel understands completely this love, because it is a reflection of the mercy of God. The image of God as loving and merciful Father is brought home in the story of the prodigal son (15:11-32). Although this story is usually called the prodigal son it is rather the story of the merciful father. It is the father who is the central figure, who gives generously and sees into the hearts of both his sons, and loves them still. This occurs especially when they need him most, even though they might not realise that need themselves. Here is a father who gives his children the freedom to go their own way, to make mistakes, and to return home to a place of mercy and love.

The Pharisees and scribes have been grumbling and complaining that tax collectors and sinners are coming near to listen to Jesus. They are horrified that Jesus welcomes sinners and, even worse, eats with them (15:2). So Jesus tells them this parable:

A Father Had Two Sons

'There was a man who had two sons. The younger of them said to his father, "Father, give me the share of the property that will belong to me." So he divided his property between them' (15:11-12).

No one can deny the appalling behaviour of the younger son. The story begins, 'Dad, why should I wait until you die before I get my inheritance? Give it to me now.' This is a shocking thing for any son to say to his father, and particularly at a time when respect for parents was central to the legal and moral code. Of the Ten Commandments, the first three deal with our relationship with God. The first of the remaining commandments – which deal with our human relationships – refers not to priest, prophet or king, but to one's own parents.

'Honour thy father and mother,' is the first rule in good human relationships. It is flagrantly broken by the younger son in Luke's parable. His demand was also unreasonable because under the progenitor inheritance laws of the time, the whole estate should go to his older brother. Also, traditional wisdom counselled against giving an inheritance before one's death. The demand made no sense. So what should the father have done? What would his hearers have expected? At least a good telling off! Instead, we hear that the father divides up the estate and gives half to the younger son. This would have been a shocking turn of events to the people of first-century Palestine.

The Dissolute Son

A few days later the younger son gathers all he has and travels to a distant country, and there he squanders his property in dissolute living. He takes all that his father generously gave to him and uses it to lead a life of self-centred indulgence, thereby losing his rights as a son.

But the good times don't last. When he has spent everything, a severe famine comes and to keep himself alive, he is forced to tend pigs. This is deeply ironic. Jewish people were forbidden to tend non-kosher animals such as pigs, so this is an acutely shameful occupation. However, things get so bad that the boy not only has to tend these swine but begins to envy them – seeking to fill his belly with the husks the pigs were eating. He has hit rock bottom.

At last the boy comes to his senses and says to himself, 'How many of my fathers' hired hands have bread enough and to spare, but here I am dying of hunger! I will get up and go to my father, and I will say to him, "Father I have sinned against heaven and before you. I am no longer worthy to be called your son. Treat me as one of your hired hands"' (15:17-19).

Luke describes how the boy 'came to himself' (15:17). That 'sensibility of heart for those in need' is awakened; the person in need is himself. Here, the first step to reparation is a merciful heart; a good sign of a merciful heart is his ability to have mercy on himself. Although he can no longer make any justified claims on his father, the boy's sober speech to himself is the first step in his return.

The Father Full of Compassion

But the father is a father and remains the father, just as the son is a son and remains the son. The son's behaviour does not diminish the father, or the father's love for his son. So the father remains faithful to himself and thereby faithful to his son. The story tells us that while the boy was still far off, his father saw him and full of compassion he rushes out to welcome his returning son and takes him in his arms. He never sent out to have him brought back. If the son wants to go his own way, the father will not stop him. He will not be forced into a life or a relationship. But there is a sense that the old man has never given up, watching and waiting for his son to return.

When he gets to the son, the father does not ask him where he has been or what happened to the money. When the son begins the rehearsed speech, the father cuts across him, turns to his servants and urges them to get a ring, sandals, and robe for his son and 'get the fatted calf and kill it, and let us eat and celebrate; for this son of mine was dead and is alive again; he was lost and is found!' (15:23). Meat was not often eaten in those days, so killing the fatted calf is a sign of special celebration. He then takes the son into the house and the party begins.

By his actions, the father bestows on him not only the forgiveness the son had hoped for; he reinstates him as a son. The father's mercy exceeds every anticipated measure. His mercy takes its bearings not from any human notion of fair allocation of material goods, but from the incomprehensible mercy of God.

There is no further mention of the younger son in the story. But this story is not so much about the son as about the father, and it doesn't finish here.

The Elder Son

Eventually, the elder son comes in, having worked in the fields all day. He is faithful and hard working. He hears the music and dancing and asks what is going on. One of the hired hands replies: 'your brother has come, and your father has killed the fatted calf, because he has got him back safe and sound' (15:27). The older son becomes angry and refuses to go in.

In those days, refusal to share a meal with one's father was a very serious matter and to do so because of resentment against one's brother would have been a very poor reason. The father comes out to plead with the son. This final conversation unveils the depths of the truly merciful heart. It contains a message as challenging for us today as it was for the people of first-century Palestine.

Remember this story is being told to the scribes and Pharisees who have been complaining that Jesus eats with sinners and is willing to sit at table with them (15:1-3). The elder son complains bitterly to his father: 'Listen! For all these years I have been working like a slave for you, and I have never disobeyed your command; yet you have never given me even a young goat so that I might celebrate with my friends. But when this son of yours came back, who has devoured your property with prostitutes, you killed the fatted calf for him!' (15:29-30). Notice the rent in the human relations: by using the phrase 'this son of yours' the elder son distances himself not only from his brother, but also from his father. But the father immediately closes the gap.

The father answers, 'Son, you are always with me.' Everything I have is yours but, 'we had to celebrate and rejoice, because this brother of yours was dead and has come to life; he was lost and has been found' (Lk 15:32). He is still your brother, my son. We have to celebrate. The words reflect a picture of mercy we might find difficult to imitate.

It is likely that most of us can identify much more easily with the elder son. He was good and loyal, dutifully serving his father without thought of personal reward. Naturally, he feels strong resentment at the extraordinary treatment his 'black sheep' of a brother gets. How can the father act like this? It doesn't seem fair.

Remember the Context

It is important for us to remember the context in which Jesus tells this story. The passage opens by saying, 'the tax collectors and sinners were coming near to listen to Jesus' (15:2). By the standards of the day, a good person avoided bad company. It was simply not acceptable to the Pharisees and Scribes, the 'good and righteous' members of the community, that this man welcomed sinners and included them at his table.

The Pharisees thought they knew who God was, and how God acts. They believed in God as law giver. God cares for the law and if you step outside the law, then you step outside God. But Jesus turned this upside down, saying that no one is outside the love of God. Even tax collectors and women working in prostitution are loved as much as those who keep the law; the sun shines on them just as much as anyone else. God's love is faithful and eternal.

God is not interested in the past but only in the present. The story challenges us to consider the nature of our relationship with God and with those around us. In wanting to experience God's mercy, we also need to learn how to be merciful to others.

The Lord asks us above all *not to judge* and *not to condemn*. If anyone wishes to avoid God's judgement, he should not make himself the judge of his brother or sister. Human beings, whenever they judge, look no farther than the surface, whereas the Father looks into the very depths of the soul ... To refrain from judgement and condemnation means, in a positive sense, to know how to accept the good in every person and to spare him any suffering that might be caused by our partial judgement, our presumption to know everything about him. But this is still not sufficient to express mercy. Jesus asks us also to *forgive* and to *give*. To be instruments of mercy because it was we who first received mercy from God.[32]

To be reconciled with God we need to learn how to be reconciled with all those who are sources of conflict or pain in our lives.

In many ways, the father's mercy extends even more profoundly to his older son who stands outside, incapable of rejoicing, feeling hurt and resentful. His judgement is severe in light of the father's boundless mercy. He too needs to be brought back into the fold.

This is a story about the incomparable love and mystery of God as father. The older son complains that his father's behaviour is absurd and unfair. The father does not dispute this. These complaints are not important. The father is not as concerned with justice as he is with mercy and unconditional love.

The Mercy of Fathers

How difficult it can be for fathers to express mercy and love is a theme down through the ages. When Lady Mary of *Downton Abbey* berates her father for 'never sticking up' for her, Robert replies, 'you are my darling daughter and I love you, hard as it is for an Englishman to say the words.' The father of the Prodigal Son is remarkably articulate in this regard. But there are other ways of expressing mercy.

Team Hoyt

Rick Hoyt suffered from oxygen deprivation at the time of his birth, and as a result was diagnosed as a spastic quadriplegic with cerebral palsy. His parents, Dick and Judy, were advised to institutionalise him because there was little hope of Rick living a 'normal' life. Instead, Dick and Judy began the quest for Rick's inclusion in community, in sports and education, and one day in the workplace. When Rick was fifteen he told his father that he wanted to participate in a five-mile benefit run for a lacrosse player who had been paralysed in an accident. Dick agreed to push Rick in his wheelchair and, while they finished next to last, they completed all five miles.

That night, Rick told his father, 'Dad, when I'm running, it feels like I'm not handicapped.' Following that, 'Team Hoyt' went on to complete one thousand races, including marathons, dualthons and triathlons. Also adding to their list of achievements, Dick and Rick biked and ran across the United States, completing a full 3,735 miles in forty-five days. Rick was once asked, if he could give his father one thing what would it be? Rick responded, 'The thing I'd most like is for my dad to sit in the chair and I would push him for once.'

Mercy: faithfulness between individuals that results in human kindness.

The Son of God and of Mary

The arrival of the Christ child is one of the great mysteries of the Christian tradition. Luke introduces Jesus through the person of his mother Mary. God's plan of salvation had been anticipated, prepared for and promised for thousands of years through the ancient people of Israel. All the great prophets – Isaiah, Jeremiah, and others – had written with hope of this promised Messiah. The fulfillment of all this promise began without fanfare or celebration with an announcement to an unknown young girl in the small country of Palestine occupied by the mighty forces of Rome in the first century.

The angel Gabriel visited Mary in Galilee, and greeted her with these words, 'Greetings, favoured one! The Lord is with you.' Mary's reaction was to be 'much perplexed' (1:28-29). Why was an angel of God coming to her? What could it mean and what did the angel want? We must remember that she was only a young girl, probably in her teens, and betrothed but not yet married to Joseph, the local carpenter. The angel sensed her unease and said: 'Do not be afraid, Mary, for you have found favour with God. And now you will conceive in your womb and bear a son, and you will name him Jesus,' also 'called the Son of the Most High' (1:31-32).

Mary said to the angel, 'How can this be, since I am a virgin?' We can only imagine the questions swirling around in Mary's head. Gabriel responds: 'The Holy Spirit will come upon you, and the power of the Most High will overshadow you; therefore the child to be born will be holy; he will be called Son of God' (1:34-35).

Mary's Response

What an amazing announcement to Mary: her son would be called the Son of God. Did she have any inkling of what this might mean or would the full realisation come only with the years? Despite the fear and confusion surrounding the angel's message, she answered 'Yes', reassured by the angel's words, 'for nothing will be impossible with God' (1:37). She was also reassured by the great news that her friend and cousin Elizabeth had conceived a son in her old age.

Mary responded, 'Here am I, the servant of the Lord; let it be with me according to your word' (1:38). She was to bear the Son of God though this would mean being pregnant before she was married – something frowned upon in her time and culture. And still she said, 'Yes.' Mary's 'yes' made it possible for God to come into the world as a human person. In this manner, by her great 'yes', Mary took on the mission which was part of God's plan for the world. She gave herself and her life to her Son and his work.

As perplexing as that news was to her when the Angel Gabriel announced it, she later rejoiced, saying:

My soul magnifies the Lord,
  and my spirit rejoices in God my Saviour,
for he has looked with favour on the lowliness of his
    servant.
  Surely, from now on all generations will call me
    blessed ...
He has helped his servant Israel,
  in remembrance of his mercy,
according to the promise he made to our ancestors,
  to Abraham and to his descendants forever. (1:
    46-55)

The Magnificat is Mary's great hymn of praise to God. She sings of God's mercy and justice to humankind. It is a song of thanksgiving for the gifts of the Lord and the joy of being loved by the Lord. The thanksgiving and joy in the hymn are closely linked to the action of God who liberates the oppressed and humbles the powerful.

It is the last time we see Mary unambiguously happy.

Mary's initial years as mother to Jesus are anything but straightforward. She gives birth in impoverished conditions, flees from a murderous ruler and becomes a refugee in a strange country. Mary also has to live with the awful prophecy of Simeon, the 'righteous and devout' man of the temple, on whom the Holy Spirit rests (2:25), who tells her: 'This child is destined for the falling and the rising of many in Israel … and a sword will pierce your own soul too' (2:34-35).

On the other hand, life settles down after the family returns to Nazareth, except for the notable incident where Jesus stays behind in the temple in Jerusalem.

The Incident in Jerusalem

Every parent can imagine something of what Mary must have felt when she and Joseph realise they had left their twelve-year-old son behind in the big city of Jerusalem. Jesus' parents do not know where he is for three days. They finally discover Jesus chatting in the temple. Understandably, Mary is vexed at his apparent lack of regard over the whole affair: 'Child, why have you treated us like this? Look, your father and I have been searching for you in great anxiety' (2:48).

The reproof is turned back upon them. Their son has two answers. First, 'why were you searching for me?'; in other words they should have known where he would be; and second, that he was about his father's business: 'did you not know that I must be in my Father's house?' (2:49). They should have known that, too!

What mother would not feel heartache at such a prophetic response from a twelve-year-old? But whatever their parenting tactics, they seem to have worked. Jesus returned to Nazareth with Mary and Joseph and is 'obedient to them' (2:51).

Life for Mary and Her Son

For Mary and her family, life gently follows the rhythm of the Nazareth seasons. Jesus learns his trade as carpenter from Joseph and lives a quiet life for thirty years. We do not know the circumstances that kept Jesus in Nazareth for all that time. What we do know is that it is his mother who encourages him to start out on his mission. She must have known, as most mothers know, that once he left, he would never really return home. But a critical event one day changes everything and she knows his time has come. It happens at the wedding feast at Cana (John 2:1-11). Mary must have been very close to the wedding party because she seems to feel their embarrassment when they run out of wine. She brings this dilemma to Jesus' attention, overrules his hesitation, and tells the servants to obey his instructions. 'My time has not yet come' her son protests. But she knows it has.

'And a Sword will Pierce your Own Soul Too'

Although there were many good years, Mary pays a heavy price for her 'yes' to God. Eventually word comes to her that Jesus has been seized. Her son is arrested, forced through a mock trial, scourged and executed. We know that she is in Jerusalem during his trial, his tortuous journey to Golgotha, and his execution. What mother wouldn't, in the words of C.S. Lewis, 'crawl through the sewers' to be with her captured child?

At the end, she stands at the foot of the cross. Where else would she be, this woman who once bathed and fed him, checked him for fevers, nursed his bruised knees and cut fingers, and gave him the push he needed when it was time for him to leave home? The sword had pierced her soul.

Mothers of the Plaza de Mayo

'I'm going out for a moment. Be right back.' Those were the last words Uranga Almeida ('Taty') heard from her son, Alejandro. It was 17 June 1975.

She never saw him again, never found out what happened to him. He became one of the 'disappeared,' the term used for those taken but never found during the military dictatorship in Argentina between the 1970s and early 1980s. This era, known as the Dirty War, represents a time of political violence during which lives were taken, families broken, and numerous atrocities committed. Human rights groups estimate that more than thirty thousand people were kidnapped and murdered during this time by extremist right-wing groups or the military government that seized power in a coup in 1976. Most of the victims' remains have never been found.

The Mothers of the Plaza de Mayo (*Asociación Madres de Plaza de Mayo*) is an association of mothers whose children were disappeared during this time. It began when a small group of mothers came together to push for information on the whereabouts of their children. Trying to learn what had happened, they gathered one Thursday, 30 April 1977, and began to walk around the Plaza de Mayo – the central square in front of the presidential palace in Buenos Aires.

'It was a woman I knew, whose son was in prison, who told me ... that some mothers of political detainees were going to the Plaza de Mayo ... to ask the authorities for information on the whereabouts of their children,' explains Hebe de Bonafini, president and co-founder of the Mothers of the Plaza de Mayo. Her son had been arrested two months earlier by the security forces. 'We went to the square that Thursday with the intention of handing over a letter to [military ruler Jorge] Videla. I remember there was a small group of mothers, some were terrified. Many of us came from small towns outside the city. Some, like me, hadn't even finished primary school. Others couldn't even read or write,' she says.

Their inquiries were met with silence. Officials refused to meet them or tell them where their children were. The authorities had forbidden public gatherings of more than three people, so the police immediately approached the group demanding they clear the square. 'But, by absolute chance, in response we started grabbing each other in pairs, arm to arm, and started walking in circles around the square. There was nothing illegal about that,' says Ms de Bonafini.

Every Thursday since 1977, the mothers have walked around the Plaza de Mayo. Together, the women created a dynamic and unexpected force, which existed in opposition to traditional limitations on women and motherhood in Latin America. With their white headscarves, the group has become known around the world.

Efforts to Stop the Group

By the end of 1977, the government response was to try to stop the mothers from gaining more recognition, especially outside Argentina. Leading members and supporters of the group were abducted and murdered.

Ms de Bonafini's own struggle intensified. Her second son was seized by the security services. Her daughter-in-law was arrested some months later. She never saw any of them again. 'I don't remember being afraid. Maybe I was just thoughtless. But it is the same mentality I had when I gave birth to my children. You don't think about the pain, you only want them to be ok.'

Sadly, every week the numbers of mothers increased. 'They touched the most sacred thing a woman can lose, a son. I was forty-five-years-old when they took Alejandro. I'm almost eighty now and I don't know what happened to him. I've been waiting all this time,' says 'Taty' Almeida.

Not many mothers who started this movement are alive today. And many of those who are alive face constant health issues because of their age. But those who can still walk every Thursday as the Mothers have done for thirty-eight years.

The Most Sacred Thing a Woman Can Lose

Mary endured the darkest night of the cross with her son. 'In the end, according to countless artistic representations of the Pietà, she held the battered body of her dead son on her lap – the most grievous experience of anguish that can befall a mother.'[34] Tragically, countless mothers down through the ages can identify with Mary in that situation. Since the earliest days of Christianity, people have identified with Mary as mother of mercy who knows the experience of suffering. The oldest Marian prayer known in Latin as *Sub tuum Praesidium* was first found on a Greek papyrus, c. 300:

> We fly to thy mercy,
> O Mother of God.
> Listen to our prayers
> and help us in our needs.[35]

The Pietà developed in Germany about 1300, and reached Italy about 1400. More recent Pietàs are adaptations of the original theme, such as Joseph Whitehead's 'Mother and Son', erected in Woodside Cemetery, Paisley, Scotland as a monument to a soldier killed in World War I.

In these representations, Mary is presented as the mother of all who are suffering, sorrowful, and in need of consolation. The most famous example, by Michelangelo, is located in St Peter's Basilica in the

Vatican City. It is different from earlier Pietà statues, not least because the body of Christ and the face of his youthful mother are things of deliberate beauty. She sits in repose, the pain and anguish of her son's torment vanished. It is as if the fullness of mercy has settled deep into that place where her soul was pierced. Human beauty, in its perfection, reflects something of the divine.

Although different cultures interpret Mary in different ways, it remains the case that remembering her as mother of mercy, drawing on her example and asking for her prayers and intercession is a deeply rooted and abiding characteristic of the Catholic community. Throughout the ages people have reached out to her, looked for her counsel and help, and asked for her prayers. In the artistic world, she remains a subject and source of inspiration.

Mercy and Children

The arrival of a child is an extraordinary gift. Many parents are amazed when they see their newborn infant; the tiny fingernails, the wispy hair, the nose, the toes … how did this little person come to be? There are often no words to express the sense of wonder and awe at this new arrival. For many, it is a profoundly spiritual experience and can deepen awareness of the pro-creative power of God at work in the world. In a culture edging towards the phenomenon of 'cotton wool kids,' we can easily lose sight of the fact that children must be allowed to live their own lives.[36] Poet Kahlil Gibran describes how our children will 'charter areas we are not even aware of.'

Parents and Children

On Children

They come through you but not from you,
And though they are with you yet they belong not to
you.

You may give them your love but not your thoughts,
For they have their own thoughts.
You may house their bodies but not their souls,
For their souls dwell in the house of tomorrow,
which you cannot visit, not even in your dreams.
You may strive to be like them,
but seek not to make them like you.
For life goes not backward nor tarries with yesterday.

You are the bows from which your children
as living arrows are sent forth.

The archer sees the mark upon the path of the infinite,
and He bends you with His might
that His arrows may go swift and far.
Let your bending in the archer's hand be for gladness;
For even as He loves the arrow that flies,
so He loves also the bow that is stable.[37]

Kahlil Gibran

In his final phrase, Gibran counsels what is best for us
as parents: 'even as [the archer] loves the arrow that
flies, so He loves the bow that is stable.' Part of merciful
parenting is allowing children to grow into themselves.
The best we can do is to give them the skills, attitudes
and dispositions to live that life well. We try to offer
stability, reliability, and a steady, merciful love.

Mercy Rebounds

The deep well of a parent's mercy is an extraordinary gift to a child; that much is clear. But it is not all a one-way street. Children, from the moment of their first smile, imitate the behaviour of their parents. A baby's first smile is usually in response to a smiling parent. Development of language is in imitation of the talk and chat among those closest to the child. It is just so with the influence of mercy. The mercy of a parent rebounds in many and unexpected ways. Children respond to that gift in childlike kind.

For children to have some sense of their responsibilities, as well as their rights, researchers such as Sharon Parks suggest that the witness of parents is the strongest influence. The behaviour of significant others is one of the most influential factors on behaviour. Initially, that influence is housed primarily in the family. As children grow up and the circle of influence spreads, community becomes increasingly important. We move on to explore the potential of community to be merciful and the effects of a merciful community.

CHAPTER THREE
Standing Together: The Call to Merciful Community

My four-year-old son wants a different name. It's not that he doesn't like his own name; he just wants a different one. 'What sort of name?' I ask. 'Hercules' is the reply – clear, definite, uncompromising. I am to go into playschool tomorrow and tell his teacher that his name is now Hercules. I know he won't thank me for it in the long run. I try to kick for touch.

'Why Hercules?'

'He has a sword, and a shield, and a flying horse' (at least in the Disney version).

I search my mind for a convincing counter argument. I think of all the thought we put into his name, the biblical resonances, how it fits so perfectly in the family. None of that will wash. How can I compete with a flying horse? I mentally rehearse the conversation I will have with Mrs O'Brien tomorrow morning. It's not going well.

To break the stalemate, we put on the movie (for the umpteenth time). There he is – half mortal, half God. Of the Gods, but not one of them, Hercules has to earn his right to a place on Olympus. And yet he doesn't fit into the human world either. The lyrics of the theme song say it all. Hercules sings that he has dreamed of a place where a great warm welcome will be waiting for him, the place where he is meant to be. I would go almost anywhere, he says, to feel like I belong.

Despite his magnificent strength and superhuman talents, Hercules doesn't belong anywhere. He has no community to send him forth or welcome him home. He has no home and no family. There is nobody with whom to make hot chocolate, or read a bedtime story, or curl up and watch a Disney movie on a wet November evening.

My conversation with Mrs O'Brien is put on hold.

The need to belong is central to human make-up. I remember a very experienced midwife once advising that a baby's greatest fear is that of abandonment. Many children are fortunate to be born into warm, welcoming communities. But that is not true for everyone. Others don't manage to put down roots until later in life. And some, like Hercules, never feel like they belong.

Standing Outside

Zacchaeus doesn't belong either. The name 'Zacchaeus' means pure or innocent. A chief of tax collectors, his task is to make sure that those under him are fully taxing the Jewish people for the benefit of the Roman Empire. Tax collectors played a role in the Roman bureaucracy that many Jews regarded as treacherous to their law. Taxation for and by the Roman Empire was considered a serious and blasphemous insult against the sovereignty of a people who considered themselves God's chosen people. Fellow Jews, who collaborated with the hated Roman regime, were despised and shunned as traitors and public sinners. To add insult to injury, Zacchaeus was a rich man; it would be easy to suspect that he acquired his wealth through an abuse of his function.

In the eyes of his fellow Jews, Zacchaeus is a traitor on two counts: a traitor to his name and a traitor to his nation. He is small not just in physical stature (19:3), but also in social standing; he has no place in the crowd which has its back to him; he is no more than a social outcast.

But he wants to see 'who Jesus was' (*et quaerebat videre Iesum quis esset* 19:3). The emphasis in the original is interesting. This is not simply a passing glance from a vaguely curious bystander. Zacchaeus wants to know what kind of a person this Jesus is. The outcast wants to see Jesus at his core. But there is an obstacle to his goal, the crowd stands in his way, so he climbs a sycamore tree (19:4).

It is interesting that Zacchaeus climbs a sycamore fig tree. These trees host all kinds of parasitic animals and insects. It suggests that the small man is like a tiny parasite feeding on his own people. Luke clearly wants to portray Zacchaeus as someone the general Jewish public would condemn as worthless and beyond mercy.

But Jesus goes to the spot where the small man is partially hidden, and calls him out by name. Zacchaeus wanted to see Jesus; he did not expect that Jesus would want to see him. But Jesus looks in his direction and says, 'Zacchaeus, hurry and come down; for I must stay at your house today' (19:5). There is an immediacy, and a divine necessity to the invitation ('I must stay … today'). It is an invitation that Jesus constantly extends to us. In calling him by name and staying at his house, Jesus bestows on him an honour for the goodness he knows is in his heart. Here, acutely, is that 'sensibility of heart for those in need.' Jesus takes the initiative; the healing and reconciliation has begun.

Zacchaeus' response is immediate and generous. He can hardly believe his ears. He rushes down and delightedly welcomes Jesus into his house. Immediately those around began to grumble: 'He has gone to be the guest of one who is a sinner' (19:7). Of all the people in Jericho, Jesus picks the house of the one person in the town who is regarded as a social and religious outcast. But his public display of mercy presents a challenge to the gathered crowd.

We are confronted with the classical reaction of the crowd to God's mercy to those who, in their estimation, don't deserve it. Whereas the crowd will claim God's mercy for themselves, they deny it to others who, in their judgement, deserve nothing other than condemnation. But Jesus sees into the heart of Zacchaeus and calls forth the goodness at his core.

As a result, Zacchaeus the chief tax collector is ready to give half of his property to the poor and, if he has cheated anyone, he promises to pay them back four times what they lost (19:8). Fourfold restitution was demanded by Jewish law, but in one case only, the theft of a sheep (Exodus 21:37). Roman law demanded restitution from all convicted thieves. Zacchaeus, however, promises to pay in any case of injustice for which he has been responsible.

Jesus always sees the real person and goes beyond the image. With just a little encouragement, Zacchaeus makes a promise from the heart, one of compassion, justice and mercy. Zacchaeus, who wanted to see, has himself been seen. The scales have fallen from his eyes. That seeing changes his whole life. But that is only half the story. Despite his heartfelt promise, the reintegration of the outcast depends on the mercy of the community.

The challenge to become a merciful community is implied in the final verses. Jesus tells Zacchaeus that 'salvation' – welcome into God's kingdom or universal culture of mercy – has come to his house (19:9). In spite of his despised profession he is 'a son of Abraham' (19:9) because his behaviour is totally in harmony with the requirements of the law and in fact goes well beyond it. No social status within or outside the community can prevent this. To be a son of Abraham is to be a loving, caring person full of compassion and a sense of justice, and not just a keeper of ritualistic observances. In other words, it is to be a person of mercy.

A People Devoid of Mercy

In F. Scott Fitzgerald's enduring masterpiece *The Great Gatsby*, the party-going set of West Egg live the decadent life of the Roaring Twenties – a mindless, indulgent, irresponsible lifestyle where consequences are just an afterthought. The privileged use their wealth and position to do as they please, without any real thought for others. Fitzgerald uses the characters of Tom and Daisy Buchanan to expose this life and its blind selfishness. They and their set are utterly oblivious to the effect their casual living has on the lives of others. Although they are constantly surrounded by 'friends', relationships are flat and connections loose. Nothing and nobody will disrupt their louche and self-protective instincts.

> They were careless people, Tom and Daisy - they smashed up things and creatures and then retreated back into their money or their vast carelessness or whatever it was that kept them together, and let other people clean up the mess they had made.[38]

Tom and Daisy run away from difficulties, mostly because they have the money to do so and they have little sense of obligation to others. In the novel, their thoughtless living leads to figurative and literal death. Four thousand years ago, the prophet Amos warned of much the same. Hear this word, he says, you who live with arrogance, heedless of others:

> Therefore, because you trample on the poor
>   and take from them levies of grain,
> you have built houses of hewn stone,
>   but you shall not live in them;
> you have planted pleasant vineyards,
>   but you shall not drink their wine …
>
> Seek good and not evil,
>   that you may live (Amos 5:11,14).

Our relative wealth can make us complacent. How easy it is to live life at the surface and to forget those around us, especially those who are in need. But for a community to function authentically, it must have mercy at its core.

The Issue of Wealth

It is important to note that in Scripture, wealth of itself is not an evil that is to be shunned. As a matter of fact, we find in the Hebrew Scriptures many instances where material wealth is bestowed on people who try to please Yahweh and respect his wishes. Job, King Solomon, Jotham and Hezekiah are all rewarded in this way. There is certainly no condemnation of the wealthy simply because they are wealthy. It is how we go about managing our wealth, whatever that 'wealth' is, that has a bearing on our lives and relationships.

Wealth can be a hindrance or a help to a merciful community. We can use our 'riches' for the good of others, or use others to enrich ourselves. Wealth in its many forms can build gates or bridges. In Luke's Gospel, Jesus' greatest condemnation is for the rich man in the story of the rich man and Lazarus (16:19-31). The rich man is excluded, not because he is rich or is personally responsible for the plight of Lazarus, but because he does absolutely nothing to help him. He exercises no mercy (sensibility of heart for those in need).

A Reversal of Fortune

In this story we meet a rich man dressed in purple and fine linen, both signs of great wealth. He keeps a sumptuous table laden with the choicest of foods. At the same time, lying on the other side of his gate, is a poor man called Lazarus. (In spite of all his wealth, the rich man is nameless). Lazarus is hungry; he longs to pick up even the scraps that fall from the dining table. He is too weak to fend off the dogs that come and lick his sores (16:19-21) – a particular humiliation.

What is striking about this scene is the sense that this is simply the way it is – the rich man eating; the poor man sitting and waiting. There is no conversation or connection between them. The poor man is not abused or chased away; he is simply ignored as if he did not exist. It depicts a stark absence of mercy.

The story centres on the reversal of fortunes that takes place after Lazarus and the rich man die. Lazarus is brought by angels to be with Abraham; the rich man is condemned to an existence of great suffering in Hades, the place of the dead. The rich man begs for even the slightest relief from the man he ignored in his lifetime. But it is too late. This reversal is ultimate. An unbridgeable chasm exists between Lazarus at Abraham's side and the rich man in Hades.

This is not the first time that Luke has described the way the status of the rich and the poor is reversed in the kingdom of God. In fact, it is a particular focus of his Gospel. When Mary receives the news from Gabriel that she is to be mother to the Son of God, she exults that the hungry have been filled and the rich sent away empty (1:46-55). In the Sermon on the Plain, Jesus tells the poor that God favours them and that the kingdom of God belongs to them, but he warns the rich that they have already received their consolation in this life (6:20-25). This is about freedom of choice – the freedom to be generous and compassionate or selfish with what we have.

The wealthy may store up treasures for themselves, but they are not 'rich toward God' (12:21). Being rich toward God and having treasure in heaven has something to do with seeing those in need and showing mercy.

The rich man had his chance and he ignored it. He had his life of 'good things' but the fine clothes and food seem very unimportant now. It is Lazarus' turn to have the really good things, the comfort and companionship of his God. When it comes to the end, life is measured not by wealth, status, or power but in a life of merciful relationships. Those are truly rich who enrich the lives of others.

The rich man then pleads on behalf of his brothers that they receive some warning. If someone would come from the dead, they would change their ways. 'They have Moses and the prophets' (the whole religious tradition) replies Abraham (16:29). 'If they do not listen to Moses and the prophets, neither will they be convinced even if someone rises from the dead' (16:31).

This parable is not so much a matter of wealth and poverty, but a matter of how that wealth is used. The rich man builds his own chasm between himself and Lazarus in the form of a gate (16:20.26). But in God's kingdom – the universal culture of mercy – the rich man and Lazarus needed each other at the table. Living as selfish independents or in self-selected compounds is a barrier to the type of inclusive community where everybody grows in mutual benefit.

But rather than showing a 'sensibility of heart to those in need,' the rich man is simply indifferent.

The story of the rich man and Lazarus might be difficult to grasp for many in the Western world whose lifestyles stand in sharp contrast with the majority of people who live on much less. It represents a sharp rebuke not only to the great confidence we place in financial security, but also to the drastic inequities we allow to perpetuate between rich and poor. The closed community attitude and insular thinking of the kingdoms of this world stand in stark contrast to the mercy and open welcome of the kingdom of God.

A Culture of Indifference

One of the most serious threats to merciful community is a culture of indifference. It is the attitude of the rich man reflected in society at large. Pope Francis has referred time and again throughout his papacy to the lure of individualism and indifference. He continually offers the challenge to break away from being closed in on oneself and one's own little nucleus of relatives and friends. A culture of indifference arises not from ill will or malice but from eyes that won't see, ears that won't hear, hearts that won't be stirred.

What Can We Do?

The Pope's Lenten message of 2014 highlights the need to counteract this culture of indifference. The message entitled *Strengthen Your Hearts*, acknowledges the reality that, as individuals, we are tempted by indifference. On the other hand, flooded with news reports and troubling images of human suffering, we often feel our complete inability to help. What can we do to avoid being caught up in this spiral of distress and powerlessness? The solution, he says, is the merciful heart.

The pope proposes that ordinary people can do three things to push back against this culture of indifference.

First, we can pray: 'Let us not underestimate the power of so many voices united in prayer!'

Second, we can help by acts of charity. We can show concern for others by small yet concrete signs of our belonging to the one human family: 'If one member suffers, all suffer together with it; if one member is honoured, all rejoice together with it' (1 Cor 12:26). We can help by, for example, raising awareness of the issue, donating or fundraising, or giving a little of our time and gifts. The Christian faith with its long tradition of active charity offers a privileged meeting point in this regard.

Third, we can attend to our own hearts. 'The suffering of others reminds us of the uncertainty of our own lives and our dependence on God and on each other. If we humbly ask for God's grace and accept our own limitations, we will trust in the infinite possibilities which God's love holds out to us.'[39] In this way we can overcome indifference and pretensions to self-sufficiency. A merciful heart means a strong and steadfast heart, closed to the tempter but open to God. Pope Francis' prayer is for each of us to cultivate a heart which is firm and merciful, attentive and generous, a heart which can stand up to the culture of indifference.

Enriching Others

In contrast to the mindset of the West Egg set of *The Great Gatsby*, there are many communities characterised by the merciful heart that display a profound respect for humanity. *L'Arche* (Ark) is an international network of faith-based communities centred on persons with significant developmental challenges. Founded in 1964 by Jean Vanier, *L'Arche* began when Vanier invited three men with developmental challenges, physical and intellectual, to live with him in a small house in France.

The L'Arche Communities: How it All Began

In the Christmas of 1963 Jean Vanier was invited to be chaplain of a small institution called the *Val Fleuri*, which looked after men with mental disabilities. He was deeply impressed by the men there, who, it seemed to him, had a special place in God's heart. Each one seemed to have so much life, but had suffered terribly and thirsted deeply for friendship. Their desire for love touched him deeply.

Jean Vanier decided to meet the person in charge of institutions for people with disabilities in the local area. With the help of his parents and friends he bought a small house which had solid walls but needed lots of repairs. An architect called Louis Pretty agreed to come and help.

On 4 August 1964 his first guests were Raphael, Philippe and Dany. Raphael and Philippe had been placed in institutions after the death of their parents. Dany was an emotionally disturbed man who could not hear or speak.

I knew that my welcoming Philippe, Raphael and Dany was a point of no return. It was as though there was now a covenant between us. All I wanted was to create a community of which they would be the centre; to give them a family, a place of belonging, where they could grow and discover the good news about Jesus.

That day was the beginning of the *L'Arche* Communities. Today there are over one-hundred-and-thirty-five *L'Arche* communities in thirty-six countries. In these communities, people with and without disabilities share their lives in homes, workshops and day programmes, through which they develop their talents and work together to make the most of life. Rooted in Christian faith, they welcome all people, regardless of religious tradition or belief.[40]

Creating Merciful Community

It is my turn to do the football camp run. A mix-up with times has me arriving for pick up thirty minutes early. I slip discreetly to the back of a little walled off area where the children are practising. Almost immediately I spot Wolverine, the child of an old school friend who lives some distance away. We haven't seen him much lately; he really struggles with the academic side of school and has needed a lot of extra literacy tuition. But he is strong and fast and badly wants to do the camp.

Two teams line up, about fifteen opposite fifteen. One team has bright yellow velcro tags stuck to their shorts. The other faces them in parallel, forming a line of defence along the centre. The tagged players have to run through the defensive line of untagged players, who try to grab their yellow tags. As the game progresses there are more and more untagged kids in the defensive line, fewer and fewer tagged kids getting through.

I can't take my eyes off Wolverine. He is one of only five tagged kids left. He appears to know exactly what he is supposed to do. His head is down, his shoulders squared. The referee blows the whistle and he runs. The power, the speed, the determination. I spot a coach on the sideline. He is one of the dads who has been coaching Wolverine and his teammates all year. An ordinary dad helping out. He is urging Wolverine on. He claps and cheers and buoys him up for the next round.

Wolverine is now one of three tagged kids left. They face impossible odds. The whistle goes and he's off. The kids come at him from every angle, trying to grab at his tag, his clothes, every part of him. The dad-coach runs along the sideline egging him on. The other two kids get caught, but Wolverine is through – almost. At the last moment a kid twice his size appears from nowhere and chops him down. He falls instantly. After a few moments, he gets up and shakes his head. The dad-coach comes over, says something to him and gives him a high five. Other kids gather round and do the same. Wolverine smiles.

All the boys can talk about afterwards is Wolverine and his 'lightning legs'. It is still the topic of conversation when the bus to bring him home arrives. Before he leaves, I write a note to his mum and we read it together:

Wolverine was a superhero at camp today. He was strong and brave and so very fast. He was the last man standing in the game of tag.

As he heads off, he starts to read it to himself. He stops after his name. He reads it again and stops at the same place. He does it again. Finally, he stuffs the note in his pocket. I see him smiling all the way to the bus.

I think of what that coach has given him. An ordinary guy, someone else's dad, to whom football is far more than a set of skills. A man building community by volunteering his time, his skills and his mercy: faithfulness between people that results in human kindness – an act in polar opposition to a culture of indifference.

Jesus in Community

Merciful community is central to the Christian ideal of living well. The first thing Jesus does following his Baptism and period spent alone in the desert is to form a community. In Luke's account, this happens in stages. He starts with the core – Peter and Andrew, James and John. A little while later he gathers the others to form the group commonly known as the twelve apostles. We hear that as he went on through cities and villages, the twelve were with him, as well as some women: Mary called Magdalene, and Joanna and Suzanna, 'and many others' (8:3).

There is a sense that the borders of this community are porous. Individuals approach the group, often seeking some sort of healing, and linger on afterwards. People come to Jesus and Jesus goes out to people. But the core of this group is strong and loyal. 'You have stood by me in my trials,' Jesus says to the twelve as they gather for the Last Supper (22:28). Despite all of this, there are times when they too drift from the mercy so characteristic of their leader.

Who Is the Greatest?

In Luke's account, it seems Jesus is always at a meal, on his way to a meal, or coming back from a meal. At the dinner table, friends, family and sometimes strangers enjoy fellowship and discuss the events of the day. It is no wonder a rivalry that has been brewing for some time boils over during a meal (22:24-34).

This dispute occurs during the Last Supper – the setting for Jesus' final words to his disciples. They have gathered for the traditional meal to celebrate the feast of Passover. Luke places the argument just after Jesus foretells his own death. The scene is fraught with emotion: Jesus claims that one among them has betrayed him. 'You have stood by me in my trials,' he says, but the betrayer is here amongst us; 'his hand in on the table' (22:28, 21). The little group that faced rejection, resistance, hostility and threat is now beginning to splinter, fractured by individual ambition and a drift from mercy.

The disciples do not know who this person might be. So they speculate with one another: 'Who would do this?' The debate quickly spirals into a disagreement about who will be leader after Jesus is gone: 'which of them was to be regarded as the greatest' (22:24). Amazing as it seems, in the midst of Jesus' revelation about his betrayal and imminent suffering and death, the disciples are fighting over who is greatest among them.

Greatness in the Kingdom of God

In response, Jesus contrasts leadership of men and women with leadership in God's kingdom. In the human world, leadership involves the bald exercise of authority - people lord it over others. In contrast stands greatness in the kingdom of God. The greatest among the disciples will be the one who is like the youngest, the one who serves: 'rather the greatest among you must become like the youngest, and the leader like one who serves' (22:26). Jesus points to his own example, not that of the culture. This is a clear reversal of the usual roles. In the ancient world the greater person sits at table while the lesser person serves the meal. But everything that Jesus had lived and taught suggests another way.

As Jesus calls them to merciful service, he also gives them a promise. He notes their constancy; unlike the betrayer, they have stood with Jesus in his trials (22:28). In the face of pressure they have stood firm. So they will share in his kingdom of table fellowship and merciful rule (22:29-30). Of course that invitation implies a responsibility. The kingdom of God will only become the kingdom of women and men if people work towards it, if the community really does practise table fellowship and mercy for all.

The Rock Cracks Open

Jesus' words about greatness and rule come in the shadow of his death. Creating that kind of community will meet with hostility and suffering. Nothing makes this clearer than the section in which Jesus warns Peter about his coming denials and encourages him in his future role as merciful leader. In this passage, unique to Luke, there is a real urgency about Jesus as he tries to prepare Peter: 'Simon, Simon, listen! Satan has demanded to sift all of you like wheat, but I have prayed for you that your own faith may not fail; and you, when once you have turned back, strengthen your brothers' (22:31-32).

Jesus knows that Peter in particular and the disciples in general will be pulled apart. But it is the rock who will first be broken. The forces of evil will attempt to destroy the little community by striking at its core. Peter will be tested, will fail utterly and weep bitterly. But he also knows that Peter will emerge from this failure as a tower of strength.

Success is not guaranteed for those associated with Jesus. No one is immune to rejection and failure. Peter is sure that he is ready to go to prison, even to die, for Jesus. He is confident that he can face whatever comes. But reliance on one's own strength is not always enough. Peter is brave in the togetherness of a meal with friends; when the soldiers show up, he will initially take up arms to defend Jesus. But when those hostile to Jesus ask him where his allegiance lies, he crumbles. Peter's denial of Jesus comes precisely at a time when he is alone, separated from the group. Without the support of community he is at his most vulnerable.

Jesus' prediction of a triple denial before the cock crows shows that he knows Peter better than Peter knows himself. Standing up to pressure alone, without recourse to God, is deceptive. Jesus' prayer is that Peter's faith may see him through. It is a prayer that echoes through the ages. Here is a friend and advocate stepping to his defence, through the ministry of prayer, when he needs it most.

The Merciful Leader

At first glance, Peter's story is one of abject failure. When put to the test, he repeatedly denies any allegiance to the man he once proclaimed as Messiah. But Peter's failure of nerve is not a failure of heart, nor will it be permanent. There will be restoration. In fact, Peter will emerge a true leader, able to strengthen his fellow disciples, just as Jesus asked him to do.

Peter will be able to strengthen the others because he will understand how easy it is to fall. He can call on them to embrace God's mercy and prepare them to stand strong because he will have experienced all of these opportunities himself. His own sensibility of heart will enable him to strengthen the hearts of his brothers.

The Acts of the Apostles, also attributed to Luke, tells us that Peter was the unquestioned leader among the apostles after the Ascension of Jesus. Under his leadership, the group left behind began the work that Jesus had commissioned them to do. The remainder of the Acts of the Apostles details the work of Peter (along with that of Paul) in such cities as Antioch, Corinth and eventually Rome where he was martyred in about AD 64. Peter's was not a success for himself, but for his tiny community. The fledgling Christian community he left behind was strong enough not only to survive but to flourish. The merciful heart of the leader remains key to successful community where people grow in mutuality.

A Leader of Mercy

Catherine McAuley was born in North Dublin in 1778. After the deaths of her parents while she was still quite young, she came face to face with the reality of poverty. Her economic circumstances in tatters, Catherine moved from one relative to another in order to have a roof over her head. This period of her life taught her first hand of dependence on the mercy of others and on the mercy of God. In 1803 she became the household manager and companion of the Callaghans – an elderly, childless, and wealthy Protestant couple. While she was living with them she began her mission of mercy to the local poor and sick. She nursed Mrs Callaghan through a lengthy illness until she died in 1819 and when William Callaghan died three years later, Catherine became the sole residuary legatee of their estate and much of their savings.

In 1824, Catherine built a large house on Baggot Street, Dublin, as a school for poor girls and a shelter for homeless girls and women. As the number of lay workers at Baggot Street increased, so did severe lay and clerical criticism: Why did these women look like a religious order, yet not abide by the normal regulations of religious orders? What mandate had this 'upstart' Miss McAuley? Why was the 'unlearned sex' doing the work of the clergy?

Catherine and her co-workers decided to deal conclusively with the threat to their works of mercy, which by then included visiting and treating the sick poor in their homes. In 1831 Catherine and two colleagues professed their religious vows as the first Sisters of Mercy, thereby founding the congregation.

By the Spring of 1832 three hundred poor girls were attending the school on Baggot Street and countless women and girls were welcomed in the shelter. When the cholera epidemic hit Dublin claiming hundreds of lives and with people fleeing the city in fear of succumbing to the disease, she organised a team of sisters to care for the sick at an improvised hospital in Townsend Street.

In the early days her work caring for the poor, the sick and educationally disadvantaged was mostly among the people of Dublin. In time the congregation spread and became one of the largest congregations of women, not alone in Ireland, but in the world. For Catherine, it was always a concern that the community would be merciful in and of itself. She personally travelled with the founding parties, remained at least a month with each new community and wrote hundreds of affectionate letters to the sisters in the new convents.

Her life as a Sister of Mercy only spanned ten years. In that time she set up a number of foundations to respond to the needs of the poor and sick both in Ireland and England. Catherine was about to establish her first foundation in America when illness overtook her. She died in 1841.

The Community Lives On

The Sisters of Mercy worldwide still try to answer the call to mercy in evolving ways. In order to embrace the mercy at the heart of their founding charism, the sisters have pledged to ask themselves:

- In what ways might we respond anew, in hope, to our call to be a compassionate presence of God in our differing realities?
- In what ways will we deepen our understanding of the diversity that is among us?

› In what ways will we allow our place in the interdependent and interconnected community of all of life to influence us?[41]

How this call is heard and answered takes many forms, through ministries of nursing, teaching, restorative justice, addiction treatment, homelessness and shelter for those, especially women, in distress.

The call to merciful community is as insistent in the twenty-first century as it was in the first. There is no generation absolved of that call. The challenge to keep mercy at the centre of community – local or even national – is difficult enough. When we step back and consider the plight of groups of people all over the world, people who desperately need help, the challenge to mercy takes on a radically different hue. It is to this we now turn.

CHAPTER FOUR

A World in Need of Mercy: All People and All Creation

Thor and Captain America burst into the kitchen. The look on their faces stops me in my tracks.

'We saw it on TV: children with no mom or dad. The older children were trying to mind the little ones. They were running from bombs and they were scared. They had nothing to eat and nowhere safe to sleep. We saw it.'

There is silence. Six-year-old Captain America is looking at me intensely. 'We can help. Just two pounds a month. There is a number you ring. It's just two pounds a month.' The focus on his face is awful. 'The number – it's 0800 …' Somehow he has managed to recall it. He stands looking at me – so serious, so earnest. I look back at him. I lift the phone.

Superheroes appear when the world needs them most.

Mercy: sensibility of heart for those in need.

The True Cost

As I write this the summer sales are in full swing. Many of us will come away from this call to frenzied bargain hunting with things we don't need and clothes we might never wear. This year, the sales coincide with the release of *The True Cost*. A documentary on the fast-fashion industry from writer and director Andrew Morgan, the film lays bare the consequences of the massive western consumption of clothes. The aim of the film, which explores the impact of fashion on people and the planet, is to foster a more considerate approach to fashion for the sake of the people whose lives depend upon it and of the planet we call home.

Globally, it is estimated that one in six people work in the fashion industry, either directly or indirectly. Many of the lowest paid and most exploited are women. *The True Cost* quotes the statistic that the average American buys eighty new pieces of clothing a year; 97 per cent of the American market is made in the developing world. The figures for Britain are similar.

Filmed just after the Rana Plaza factory collapse in 2013 in which 1,129 workers perished, *The True Cost* tells the story of seamstresses who are separated from their children in order to work – they can't afford not to. It highlights the reality of women beaten for asking for better pay conditions, and cotton growers suffering cancer and birth defects because of pesticides used to get higher yields. According to Claudia Croft, fashion editor with *The Sunday Times*, 'it makes you look at a £10 jeans in a different way.' She goes to on to question the possible solutions: boycott clothes make in Bangladesh? Buy only clothes made locally? Wear only Fairtrade or second-hand items?[42] But these blanket strategies can also have negative consequences.

Ethical campaigner Livia Firth advises people to get off the treadmill of buying new, cheap things daily or weekly and practise slow shopping instead. Her advice is to be curious, be an active citizen, and support high street players with good records who look at the ecological consequences and social justice implications of their supply chain. In many ways, it is a call to consider the vast potential of mercy.

The Extent of the Call to Mercy

In the cars we drive, clothes we wear, food we eat, we affect the lives of others. We are interconnected in more ways than we probably realise. The culture of indifference we read about in the previous chapter takes on a whole new meaning in this context; it becomes the globalisation of indifference.

In this context, some people continue to defend trickle-down theories which assume that economic growth, encouraged by a free market, will inevitably succeed in bringing about greater justice and inclusiveness in the world. This opinion, which has never been confirmed by the facts, expresses a crude and naïve trust in the goodness of those wielding economic power and in the sacralized workings of the prevailing economic system. Meanwhile, the excluded are still waiting.

To sustain a lifestyle which excludes others, or to sustain enthusiasm for that selfish ideal, a globalisation of indifference has developed. Almost without being aware of it, we end up being incapable of feeling compassion at the outcry of the poor, weeping for other people's pain, and feeling a need to help them, as though all this were someone else's responsibility and not our own. The culture of prosperity deadens us;

we are thrilled if the market offers us something new to purchase. In the meantime all those lives stunted for lack of opportunity seem a mere spectacle; they fail to move us.[43]

An Ancient Call

At the heart of the Christian tradition is a call to exercise mercy beyond the borders of family and community. It extends way past our own nuclei to those with whom we have no apparent connection, for whom we may not wish to feel responsible. It is as far from indifference as we can imagine. An ancient biblical call, it is often referred to as 'the mercy of strangers'.

The history of Judeo-Christianity is rooted in slavery and liberation. Stretching through the Hebrew and Christian scriptures, the biblical imperative is to hold that memory in order to keep freedom a reality. 'You shall not oppress the stranger, for you know the soul of the stranger, having yourselves been strangers in the land of Egypt,' says the Book of Exodus (Ex 33:1). The letter to the Hebrews counsels, 'do not neglect to show hospitality to strangers for by doing that some have entertained angels without knowing it' (Heb 13:1). But this has never been an easy call to hear.

Amal's Story

The novel *Mornings in Jenin* by Susan Abulhawa tells the story of Amal Abulheja and her family. For countless generations her ancestors farmed the lands around Ein Hod in Northern Palestine before their dispossession in 1948. Love was plentiful in Ein Hod; love for life, for family, for God, and for the land.

> In a distant time, before history marched over the hills and shattered present and future, before wind grabbed the land at one corner and shook it of its name and character, before Amal was born, a small village east of Haifa lived quietly on figs and olives, open frontiers and sunshine.[44]

But the family and their countrymen are forced out of their villages and homes, eventually finding refuge in a camp in Jenin, where Amal is born. She grows up in the shadow of a mother devastated by the loss of a child in the flight in 1948. After the uprising of 1967, her gentle, poetry-reading father is never seen again. Her mother slips into dementia, and her brother Yousef leaves to join the resistance.

Amal's childhood is framed by a family suffering from overwhelming loss, a community which dreams of return, but eventually sends her forth, and a wider world that doesn't seem to care. A rare scholarship to a university in the United States is the reward for her bright intellect and love of reading. But the experience only heightens the chasm between her own culture and that of a careless world. Western life poses too many contradictions for Palestinians like herself. She returns to Lebanon only to have her hopes shattered all over again by the massacres at Sabra and Shatila.

Susan Abulhawa describes how on 16 September 1982, in defiance of the cease-fire, the army circled the refugee camps of Sabra and Shatila. Israeli soldiers set up checkpoints, barring the exit of refugees, and allowed their Lebanese Phalange allies into the camps, where they went from shelter to shelter. Two days later, the first western journalists entered the camp and bore witness. Robert Fisk wrote of it in *Pity the Nation*:

> They were everywhere, in the road, the laneways, in the back yards and broken rooms, beneath crumpled masonry and across the top of garbage tips. When we had seen a hundred bodies, we stopped counting. Down every alleyway, there were corpses–women, young men, babies and grandparents–lying together in lazy and terrible profusion where they had been knifed or machine-gunned to death. Each corridor through the rubble produced more bodies. The patients at the Palestinian hospital had disappeared after gunmen ordered the doctors to leave. Everywhere, we found signs of hastily dug mass graves.[45]

While we might comfort ourselves in the knowledge that Amal's story lies in the past, we need to have the courage to open our eyes and see the world as it is today. There are many children, women and men who live precariously, in dehumanising conditions; many families who live within structures that corrode rather than affirm their dignity and humanity. What does the world look like from their perspective?

Seeing the world through the eyes of those who are marginalised and suffering is difficult and it is a choice. It requires a courageous and merciful heart – a desire to see the ways in which people inflict hardship and pain on others and to identify with those who are suffering. This is the real challenge of the call to exercise 'the mercy of strangers.' Can we allow ourselves to be confronted by such a reality, to be moved by their cries? And how do we respond?

How Do We Respond?

If we return for a moment to the passage we read in the first chapter where Jesus announces that Isaiah's prophecy is fulfilled (4:16-21), we get a sense of how humanity is often tempted to respond. Initially, Jesus' proposed ministry of lifting the burden sounds like good news to his hearers in Nazareth, at least if that healing and release is meant for them. But when Jesus reminds them that God's love extends beyond their borders, that Elijah helped a woman from Sidon (4:26) and Elisha healed a Syrian (4:27), they conclude that his message is really bad news.

In order to accept his teaching, they would have to change their attitudes toward outsiders. They would have to widen their eyes and open their hearts. They would have to believe that God's mercy is really for all of humankind, and not just for them. That is more transformation than Jesus' hometown hearers can handle. In their angry desire to make God's mercy serve their own purposes, they turn on Jesus.

The Good Samaritan

For a scriptural insight into the mercy of strangers, we turn to one of the most famous of Luke's parables.

Just then a lawyer stood up to test Jesus. 'Teacher,' he said, 'what must I do to inherit eternal life?' He said to him, 'What is written in the law? What do you read there?' He answered, 'You shall love the Lord your God with all your heart, and with all your soul, and with all your strength, and with all your mind; and your neighbour as yourself.' And he said to him, 'You have given the right answer; do this, and you will live' (10:25-28).

But wanting to justify himself, he asked Jesus, 'And who is my neighbour?' (10:29).

Jesus then tells this story:

'A man was going down from Jerusalem to Jericho, and fell into the hands of robbers, who stripped him, beat him, and went away, leaving him half dead' (10:30).

The Road from Jerusalem to Jericho

In first-century Palestine, the road from Jerusalem to Jericho was the equivalent of a 'no-go area'. The seventeen-mile stretch that connects these two cities descends some 3,300 feet through desert and rocky country. Lined with caves, it provided excellent cover for robbers and bandits. The road was notoriously dangerous. Even if a man had little of value, the robbers on the Jericho Road would attack him for his clothing alone.

In Jesus' story, a man travelling this road is overcome by a band of robbers, stripped of his clothing and left on the road to die. Then a priest comes down the road. He is probably returning to Jericho (a principal residence for priests) from service in the temple at Jerusalem. The expectation culturally would be relief: surely help is on the way now. But the priest does not stop. Rather, he crosses to the other side and keeps going (10:31). The detail about crossing the road is no accident. The priest gets as far away as possible from the wounded man as he passes by.

Then a Levite, another potential source of aid, arrives on the scene. Levites were an order of cultic officials, inferior to priests but still a privileged group in society. As such, he would surely stop to help. But when he sees the man, he also crosses to the other side of the road and moves on (10:32). So two men of similar cultural background have failed to offer assistance. They see the man's need but choose not to help. They have failed to be neighbours.

No Excuses

Interpreters speculate as to why they refuse to help. Do they fear being attacked themselves? Do they fear being rendered unclean? Some believe that the priest and Levite might have had some justification for their actions. After all, as temple officials they were bound by regulations about ceremonial cleanliness. Whatever the excuse, placing religious purity over helping a person who is in dire straits is a serious misinterpretation of God's law of love.

The text gives us no reason. As is often the case, getting involved is costly, and for many the investment is too high. Walking on the other side of the road is a deliberate statement of 'I don't want to know!' The less they see about the man's condition, the less they would feel obliged to help him. But the refusal to see is as significant a failure of mercy as is the refusal to help.

But now another traveller comes on the scene. The text highlights this man's arrival by placing his ethnic identity, a Samaritan, up front. The lawyer hearing the story must be thinking, 'there will be no help from this quarter.' But as often happens in Jesus' parables, a twist on cultural expectations yields this story's major point: it is the stranger, the person unknown, from another place and of another culture, who becomes the exemplar of God's love.

The original impact of the parable of the Good Samaritan is generally lost today. After centuries of telling and re-telling, the word 'Samaritan' has become synonymous with kindness, generosity and outreach to those in need. But to the original Jewish audience, a Samaritan would have represented the exact opposite. That is an important emotive element to remember. Culturally he is the last person they would have expected to be hailed as an exemplary neighbour.

The Detested Samaritans

For historic reasons, the Samaritans were particularly hated by the Jews of Jerusalem. At times, relations between the Jews and Samaritans had been civil, but in Jesus' day feelings were definitely hostile. As John the evangelist observes: 'Jews do not associate with Samaritans' (John 4:9b).

The Samaritan doesn't cross to the other side of the road. When he sees the wounded man he takes pity on him. The word translated as 'pity' refers figuratively to the seat of the emotions (in our usage 'heart'). Compassion and mercy are motivated by the need of another, while withholding mercy is essentially an act of selfishness, of self-protection.

In minimal, focused language, Jesus details all the Samaritan does to save the man – six actions in all. He comes up to the man, binds his wounds, cares for them with oil and wine, loads him on his mule, takes him to an inn and cares for him, even paying for his stay (10:34-35). The Samaritan applies oil and wine as healing agents. Although people of the time had no knowledge of infectious disease, the cleansing and healing properties of wine were well understood. Olive oil was widely employed to protect exposed parts of the skin, to relieve chafing, to soften wounds, and to heal bruises and lacerations.

In short, the Samaritan used his own supplies to cleanse and soothe the man's wounds, his own clothing to bandage him, his own animal to carry him while the Samaritan himself walked, his own money to pay for his care, and his own reputation and credit to vouch for any further expenses the man's recovery would require. The Samaritan's mercy is a generous mercy. It doesn't just keep the letter of the law, but its spirit as well.

The Story Closes
Jesus' question to close the story requires no brilliant reply: 'Which of these three do you think was a neighbour to the man who fell into the hands of robbers?'

The lawyer knows, but he cannot bring himself to mention the man's race. It would mean extending his responsibilities, his 'choice' of neighbour. He still does not understand, or perhaps want to understand, the extent of the call to mercy. Nevertheless, he answers, *'The one who had mercy on him.'*

This reply is correct, so Jesus simply says, 'Go and do likewise.' In other words, do not rule out certain people as neighbours. Just be a neighbour whenever and wherever you are needed, and realize that neighbours can come from surprising places.

Context and Connections

The context in which Jesus tells the parable is almost as important as the parable itself. It is set in a series of three passages in which Luke addresses attitudes toward our neighbour, spending time with Jesus and praying to God. The grouping is important. It suggests connections among the various relationships. Who we see as neighbour, how we respond to our neighbours, and how we walk with God are connected.

In this passage a lawyer asks Jesus how one can inherit eternal life. This is not the kind of lawyer who goes to court to defend a client. This 'lawyer' is an expert in Jewish law, in particular, the Law of Moses, which is contained in the first five books of the Bible. In other words this person is a Scripture scholar, specialising in the Law of Moses.

As a Jewish lawyer this man knows that God exists and that he is accountable to that God. His question has a particularly focus: 'Teacher, what must I do to inherit eternal life?' (10:25). In effect he asks how he can be sure to participate in and be blessed at the resurrection of the dead. Jewish scribes had great interest in such questions, not only for personal reasons but because they were engaged in interpreting the law for the whole community.

The legal expert's answer shows much insight. He draws together two of the great Hebrew Scripture texts: 'Love the Lord your God with all your heart and with all your soul and with all your strength and with all your mind' (Deuteronomy 6:5) and 'Love your neighbour as yourself' (Leviticus 19:18).

Jesus compliments him on his response: 'You have given the right answer' (10:28). The lawyer agrees that the essence of the Torah is to love one's neighbour as oneself, but then seeks to limit the application of this to his own community. He latches on to the second part of the reply about one's neighbour. Exactly where does his responsibility fall? Does it have limits? What is your definition of 'neighbour'? he asks Jesus.

Which of These Three … Was a Neighbour to the Man?

Jesus' reply is in the form of a question: which of the three proved to be a neighbour to the wounded man (10:36)? The expert in law replies, 'the one who showed him mercy' (10:37). Mercy (Greek: eleos) from the Hebrew concept of hesed, faithfulness between individuals that results in human kindness.

Jesus doesn't define 'neighbour' in so many words, but his story makes it clear that our neighbour is whoever has a need. It is a question of opening our eyes. Jesus' command to love our neighbour as ourselves knows no self-satisfying limits.

Go and Do Likewise

Remember that the lawyer's question relates to what one must do to inherit eternal life. He has offered the correct answer himself: to love God with everything you have, all you are made of, and to love your neighbour as yourself. In the final exchange between the two, Jesus challenges him to do just that: 'go and do likewise' (10:37). Know mercy and show mercy, and then you know fullness of life and the joy of living.

When Jesus says, 'Do this and you will live,' he is saying that relationship with God is what gives life. The chief end of humankind is to love God wholly. Here is the definition of life that brings life. Everything develops from there. And the product of our love for God will be a regard for others made in God's image, even and sometimes especially those who are not immediately recognisable as neighbours. The issue is not action alone; it is also to do with disposition, the heart of the person. *'Pensar con la Corazon,'* my Spanish friend summarises: 'we need to think with the heart'. When we give or receive mercy, 'otherness' ceases and we experience instead our common humanity.

Of course the opposite is also true. When we don't allow our eyes to see, our ears to hear, we are failing ourselves, our neighbours and the human soul. When we avert our eyes and cross to the other side, when we decide that 'I don't want to get involved' we are walking away from humanity. But it comes at a cost to our own souls.

Part of our nature is to be neighbour. When we go against human nature, when we disconnect how we act from who we really are, it precipitates a slow disintegration of our individual selves and of the human soul. In choosing not to recognise and help, we are going against what it means to be human. Rainer Maria Rilke captures this disconnect when he writes:

> Ah, not to be cut off,
> not through the slightest partition
> shut out from the law of the stars.
> The inner – what is it?
> if not the intensified sky,
> hurled through with birds and deep
> with the winds of homecoming.[46]

There is within us a yearning for connectedness, a yearning to live without the 'slightest partition' between our souls and the distant stars, between ourselves and otherness. We yearn for community with the other, because deep within we know that in true community we would feel more at home in our lives, no longer strangers to one another and to the earth.

Three Things

Luke immediately follows the parable of the Good Samaritan with his account of Jesus' visit to Martha and Mary. Both are found only in Luke and it is no coincidence that he places them back to back. The story of Martha and Mary is, in a way, a contrast to the previous one. It restores a balance. The exchange between Jesus and the lawyer about being a neighbour could lead us to think that being merciful is confined only to *doing*. The encounter with Martha and Mary emphasises that both *prayer* and *attending to one's heart* need to complement practical outreach.

Martha and Mary

When Jesus comes to Bethany, Martha welcomes him into the home she shares with her sister Mary (10:38). She then busies herself with the tasks of serving their guest (10:40). Although Luke does not describe precisely what those tasks are, the hospitality code of the culture would suggest she began preparing a meal.

Meanwhile her sister Mary sits at Jesus' feet, listening to him (10:39). Sitting with Jesus in this way is the essence of prayer.

Worry and Distraction

The story takes an unexpected turn when Martha, distracted by her many tasks, comes to Jesus and asks, 'Lord, do you not care that my sister has left me to do all the work by myself? Tell her then to help me' (10:40).

Martha was a doer to the point of distraction. An older translation of this passage tells us that she was 'burdened with much serving' (10:40). Certainly Jesus urges service to the neighbour many times; we see this clearly in the preceding parable of the Good Samaritan. But it should not be a burden. Service to others needs to rest within realistic parameters. Authentic service results from a sense of gratitude. Peter McVerry SJ, an indefatigable advocate for social justice and for the marginalised in Irish society, puts it like this:

> Gratitude to God for being loved is the only motivation worthy of a follower of Jesus. The deeper our appreciation of the love of God, the more we will want to return that love to God by reaching out to God's children, loving and caring for them, especially those most in need of love and care.[47]

The problem with Martha is not that she is busy serving, but rather that she is worried and distracted. She is being pulled or dragged in different directions. It signifies a paucity of peace, a lack of sensibility of heart.

Jesus' response reflects this disquiet within her: 'Martha, Martha, you are worried and distracted by many things; there is need of only one thing. Mary has chosen the better part, which will not be taken away from her' (10:41-42).

Because Mary seemed to be doing nothing, Martha saw her as idling and selfish. Martha must have been taken aback when Jesus said that Mary had 'chosen the better part' which would 'not be taken from her'.

Martha's distraction leaves no room for the most important aspect of hospitality – gracious attention to the guest. In fact, she breaks all the rules of hospitality by calling attention to the behaviour of her sister, and by asking her guest to intervene in a family dispute. She even goes so far as to accuse Jesus of not caring about her: 'Lord, do you not care …' (10:40).

Her worry and distraction drive a wedge between her sister and herself, and between Jesus and herself, and prevent her from being truly present with Jesus. She has missed out on the chance to spend quality time with her guest. Listening to God's message is something Jesus tells his followers they need to do all the time. The pattern of his own prayer life involves regular time apart, listening to the Father. Listening involves understanding, accepting and assimilating that message so that it becomes part of our very selves and guides us to mercy.

This story compliments the parable of the Good Samaritan which went before it. Taken together they express the essence of the Christian message – living in merciful relationship with oneself, the neighbour and with God.

The One Thing Needed

In a culture of hectic schedules and the relentless pursuit of productivity, we are tempted to measure our worth by how busy we are, by how much we accomplish, or by how well we meet the expectations of others. Feeling pulled in different directions, feeling worried and distracted by many things are common threads of life in our fast-paced world. And yet Jesus asks, 'Can any of you by worrying add a single hour to your span of life?' (12:25). We know deep down that much of what we worry about is not so important in the larger scheme of things, and yet we cannot seem to quell our anxious thoughts and frantic activity.

It is also true that much of our busyness and distraction stems from the noblest of intentions. We want to provide for our families, we want to give our children every opportunity to enrich their lives, we want to be good neighbours. And yet if all our activities leave us with no time to be still in the presence of God and hear God's word, we are likely to end up anxious and troubled. We are likely to end up devoid of love and joy and resentful of others.

Further, if we do not spend time listening to God, how can we know that our activity is properly directed? It is easy for us to be very busy but are we busy about the right things? To answer those questions we have to stop, to listen, to discern, to pray and to attend to our own hearts. Jesus' words to Martha are really an invitation: 'Martha, Martha, you are worried and distracted by many things; there is need of only one thing' (10:41). The one thing needed is for Martha to spend attentive time in the presence of God so that her heart might be a merciful one. This need is as resonant today as it ever was in light of the dangers of group think and the desensitising effect of wrongdoing.

The Numbing of Conscience

Dietrich von Hildebrand was a German Catholic thinker and teacher who devoted his intellect to breaking the deadly spell of Nazism that ensnared so many. In *My Battle Against Hitler*,[48] von Hildebrand describes how even those who are indignant when first exposed to an evil in society can become accepting of it. When seeing and hearing becomes habitual, the outrage and compassion that was our first response becomes numb.

Von Hildebrand goes on to explain how if we simply permit ourselves to get used to an evil, if we simply 'come to terms' with it because it exists de facto and we cannot change it, then our souls will suffer harm. He argues that it is imperative that we recognise this danger and take up the battle against the desensitising effect of habitual wrongdoing.

When a society suffers a failure of mercy, there can be devastating consequences. Unfortunately history is full of examples of what psychologists term 'motivational blindness' or 'bystander effect', whereby people turn a blind eye and bury the stirrings of conscience beneath excuses and hollow justifications.

A memory stirs of the scene in Harper Lee's *To Kill A Mockingbird* in which a black man, Tom Robinson, is convicted of raping a white woman. Again, it is a child who articulates the terrible reality of the situation. Jem, who is thirteen-years-old, has sat through the trial. He has seen how flimsy the evidence against Tom is, and heard the obvious truth of the defence; he cannot understand how Tom is convicted. Jem knows in his heart, and knows that the jury must also know, that Tom is innocent. He cries hot, angry tears all the way home. Atticus Finch, Jem's father, who is the defence lawyer in the case, remarks how 'it seems that only children weep.'[49]

It is not easy for people to resist cultural appeasement and remain true to their consciences. In doing so, they can find themselves out of step with their erstwhile friends and colleagues, and with society at large. But the alternative can also come at a price. The effects may not be immediately apparent, but Von Hildebrand is certain: the human soul is harmed. Living in merciful relationship with the wider world is not a one way street; it is good for our souls – our deepest selves. To reclaim ourselves and our humanity we need to open our eyes; moreover, we need to *want* to open our eyes.

A Culture Without Mercy

Without mercy, a culture of wrongdoing can become so pervasive that people accept it as inevitable. Theologians call this social sin. An entire society gets blinded into thinking something is acceptable because everyone is doing it or ignoring it or excusing it. The drug culture of the professional cycling world is a case in point. That culture blew up with the admissions of Floyd Landis, Tyler Hamilton and other cycling champions. Their stories had a common theme: to make it as a professional cyclist, you had to take drugs. Everybody was doing it. If everyone was doping then it wasn't cheating – right? But the consequences were awful.

In 1998 David Zabriskie won the *Grand Prix des Nations* cycling race in France for riders under twenty three. After the race, the manager of the US Postal Service team approached him, the man who had led Armstrong and the team to two tour victories. He offered Zabriskie a place on the Postal team; the cyclist accepted on the spot. Suddenly he found himself in Europe training and competing on the most famous tours in the world.

David Zabriskie was an excellent young cyclist. He couldn't understand when, even at his maximum, others guys were just flying by him. Within a short time it was clear that he was in danger of losing his place on the team. The team manager and the team doctor told him that to succeed in the sport he needed to start injecting EPO (a hormone that induces red blood cell production) and taping testosterone patches to his body.

Zabriskie started to ask questions. He had every reason to. His own father had been an addict and a drug dealer, sprawled all day in front of the basement TV, the air thick with stale marijuana smoke, and the place littered with empty whiskey bottles. Zabriskie had had a threatening and tumultuous childhood. Cycling had saved him. He had sworn never to do drugs but had become sucked into a world where doping was the norm. Zabriskie felt like a passenger in a plane crash without time to save himself. Looking around he wondered if there was 'anyone strong enough to resist the suffocating pressure, to stop time and walk away.'[50]

Von Hildebrand and other commentators wonder if, in our oases of comfort and convenience, we are increasingly desensitised to the failures of mercy so prevalent in our world and, indeed, in ourselves. Our world of hyper-stimulation and instant gratification can so numb the antennae of our consciences that we are increasingly unaware of or indifferent to the moral erosion and widespread injustices that threaten our society and, indeed, our humanity. This is a far cry from the universal culture of mercy that is the kingdom of God.

Mercy in the Kingdom of God

In December 2012, UN High Commissioner for Refugees António Guterres organised an international and interreligious dialogue on the theme of 'faith and protection'. In his opening remarks, Guterres noted '... all major religious value systems embrace humanity, caring and respect, and the tradition of granting protection to those in danger. The principles of modern refugee law have their oldest roots in these ancient texts and traditions.'[51] In other words, the call to show mercy to the stranger extends beyond any one religious tradition.

In response, a coalition of leading faith-based humanitarian organisations and academic institutions drafted, 'Welcoming the Stranger: Affirmations for Faith Leaders.' The founding principles of the affirmations remind us that the call to show mercy to the stranger, through protection and hospitality, and to honour those who are 'other' with respect and equality, is deeply rooted in all major religions.

In Hindu culture, the mantra *atithi devo bhava,* or 'the guest is as God', expresses the fundamental importance of hospitality. Central to the Hindu Dharma, or law, are the values of *karuna* (compassion), *ahimsa* (non-violence), and *seva* (the willingness to serve the stranger and the unknown guest).

There are many different traditions of Buddhism, but the concept of *karuna* (compassion) is a fundamental tenet in all of them. It embodies the qualities of tolerance, non-discrimination, inclusion and empathy for the suffering of others.

The Torah makes thirty six references to honouring the stranger, making it one of the most prominent tenets of the Jewish faith.

In Matthew's Gospel (Mt 32:32) we hear the call: 'I was hungry and you gave me food, I was thirsty and you gave me something to drink, I was a stranger and you welcomed me ...' The Letter to the Hebrews advises: 'do not neglect to show hospitality to strangers, for by doing that some have entertained angels without knowing it' (Heb 13:2-3).

When the Prophet Muhammad fled persecution in Mecca, he sought refuge in Medina, where he was warmly welcomed. The Prophet's *hijrah*, or migration, symbolises the movement from lands of oppression, and his hospitable treatment embodies the Islamic model of refugee protection. The Holy Qur'an calls for the protection of the asylum seeker, or *al-mustamin*, whether Muslim or non-Muslim.

In short, compassion and mercy play a central role in world religions. Yet there are tens of millions of refugees and internally displaced people in the world. To make a difference we need to get involved in some way, however small. Our faiths demand that we remember we are all migrants on this earth, journeying together in hope.

All Migrants on This Earth

In April 2015, a boat packed with migrants went down sixty miles from the Libyan coast. Almost seven hundred lives were lost – men, women and children. After learning of the disaster, Pope Francis, an outspoken advocate for greater European-wide participation in rescue efforts, reiterated his call for action. 'They are men and women like us ... seeking a better life, starving, persecuted, wounded, exploited, victims of war,' he said from St Peter's Square.

Immigration is a priority of Pope Francis' papacy. His first trip, in 2013, was to the island of Lampedusa, to pay tribute to the thousands of migrants who have died trying to cross the Mediterranean. In his homily at Mass celebrated with the residents of Lampedusa and the immigrants who have sought refuge there, Pope Francis spoke again against the 'globalisation of indifference' that leads to such tragedies.[52]

Over the last few years, thousands of migrants have drowned in the Mediterranean, amid a surge in overcrowded boats heading for Europe from places like Libya and Turkey. The vicious civil war in Syria has triggered a huge exodus, while Afghans, Eritreans and other nationalities are also fleeing war, poverty and human rights abuses. Survivors of the perilous voyage often report violence and abuse by people traffickers. Many migrants pay thousands of dollars to traffickers, only to end up abandoned on boats in the Mediterranean.

In September 2015, the body of a small Syrian child in a red T-shirt and dark shorts, was washed up on a beach in Turkey. It was three-year-old Aylan Kurdi, his cheek pressed to the sand as if he were sleeping, the waves lapping around his face. The smugglers had promised his father Abdullah Kurdi a motorboat for the trip from Turkey to Greece. It was a step on the way to a new life he hoped to build for his family with his sister in Canada. Instead, the smugglers showed up with a fifteen-foot rubber raft that overturned in high waves, throwing Mr Kurdi, his wife and their two small sons into the sea.

After it capsized, the family clung to the boat. Mr Kurdi tried to keep the boys, Aylan and Galip, afloat, but one by one they, along with his wife Rehan, died, too exhausted to keep their heads above the water. Only the father survived. 'Now I don't want anything,' he said a day later. 'Even if you give me all the countries in the world, I don't want them. What was precious is gone.'[53]

The flow of desperate migrants hoping to reach Europe has reached crisis point. Championing the rights of poor migrants is difficult as the economic climate is still uncertain, many Europeans are unemployed and wary of foreign workers, and EU countries are divided over how to share the refugee burden. When Jesus said 'go and do likewise' he never said it would be easy.

The Earth We Call Home

If Pope Francis has been an outspoken advocate for migrants, he certainly does not pull his punches when it comes to the environment. He is very clear that human responsibility to those in need extends to the planet we call home.

Much more than a warning about the abuse of the environment, the pope's encyclical of June 2015 *Laudato Si': On Care for our Common Home* is a summons to mercy. It is the mercy whose call echoes throughout Scripture, a mercy between ourselves and future generations, between ourselves and poorer nations, and between ourselves and all of creation. It is a mercy which requires not so much the sacrifice of 'the good life' as much as the embrace of those priorities which lead to 'a life that is good'. Here is what commentator Austin Ivereigh posted on the letter:

While it acknowledges and reflects the overwhelming consensus that the globe is getting warmer because of a model of growth that rests on frenetic consumption and greed ... the science, as such, occupies relatively little space in the document. Just as important is the attention given to the experience of the poorest of the world of rising seas, unstable seasons, deforestation and pollution. The evidence in the encyclical of the deteriorating quality of life across the world will be hard to refute.

What *Laudato Si'* does is link that devastation and deterioration to a model of economic growth underpinned by compulsive consumerism . . . At the heart of that mentality is a false idea of dominion. What it produces is vast waste, exploitation, and a throwaway attitude towards the planet and human life itself.

As cardinal archbishop of Buenos Aires, Jorge Mario Bergoglio was keenly aware of the way these issues interconnected. The Uruguayan paper mill at Fray Bentos which polluted the River Plate, the deforestation in Tartagal in northern Argentina that produced devastating floods, the shrinking rainforests of the Peruvian and Brazilian Amazon, and the people-trafficking that supplied the sweat shops and brothels of Buenos Aires – these were part of the same sickness.

His own integrity in this area is unquestionable. He travelled by public transport, recycled clothes, lived sparsely and simply and loved to be with the poor and the outcast. He lived as a bishop in a major modern city more or less as St Francis of Assisi did in medieval Umbria. If anyone can speak to us with authority on this issue, it is the Pope. He has walked the walk and talked the talk for decades.[54]

Laudato Si' is a lament for a lost connectedness, and a passionate plea for the restoration of merciful relationships: with God, with each other, with our deepest selves and with the earth. It demands of us the mercy that is at the heart of Christianity.

Our Responsibility to the Natural World

As with most responsibilities, looking after the created world is not a one-way street. The gift of rest and renewal that we receive from nature has been a common theme of artists, writers and musicians over the centuries. For Charles Dickens, the natural world provided an antidote to the overcrowded, sickly, smog ridden city. In his time, England was rapidly becoming an industrial, urban society. It is in a peaceful country village that *Oliver Twist* begins to recover from the effects of his tormented childhood:

> Who can describe the pleasure and delight, the peace of mind and soft tranquillity, the sickly boy felt in the balmy air and among the green hills and rich woods of an inland village! Who can tell how scenes of peace and quietude sink into the minds of pain-worn dwellers in close and noisy places, and carry their own freshness deep into their jaded hearts! ... [B]ut beneath all this, there lingers, in

the least reflective mind, a vague and half-formed consciousness of having held such feelings long before, in some remote and distant time, which calls up solemn thoughts of distant times to come, and bends down pride and worldliness beneath it.[55]

In this passage, Dickens claims outright not just physical but spiritual benefits of the rural environment. The natural world connects us to our better selves, to humanity and ultimately to the divine. As creatures on this earth we are all interconnected. Albert Einstein expresses it like this:

A human being is a part of the whole called by us universe, a part limited in time and space. He experiences himself, his thoughts and feeling as something separated from the rest . . . This delusion is a kind of prison for us restricting us to our personal desires and to affection for a few persons nearest to us. Our task must be to free ourselves from this prison by widening our circle of compassion to embrace all living creatures and the whole of nature in its beauty.[56]

Mercy – sensibility of heart for those in need.

We have seen from the parable of the Good Samaritan and the story of Martha and Mary that the issue of mercy is not one of action alone; it is also to do with disposition (the merciful heart of the person), and with guidance through prayer. The merciful self, merciful communities and participating in a merciful world are all rooted in the mercy of God. Fullness of life is in the interdependence of these relationships. For Christians, the mercy of God towards humanity and creation is the starting point. Everything else grows out from that relationship. It is to that relationship we now turn.

CHAPTER FIVE

The Great Unknown: Relationship with God Who is Mercy

When high school teacher Caelum Quirk and his wife, Maureen, a school nurse, move to Littleton, Colorado, they both get jobs at Columbine High School. In April 1999, while Caelum is away, Maureen finds herself in the library at Columbine, expecting to be killed as two vengeful students go on a carefully premeditated, murderous rampage.

When the shooting begins in the Columbine library, Maureen crawls inside a cabinet and writes Caelum a goodbye note. Although of no particular faith tradition and with little knowledge or practice of prayer, somewhere from deep within her, she hears herself praying fragments of the Hail Mary. She prays it over and over again until the shooting stops. Miraculously, she survives, but at a cost: she is unable to recover from the trauma. When Caelum and Maureen flee to an illusion of safety on the Quirk family's Connecticut farm, they discover that the effects of chaos are not easily put right, and further tragedy ensues.

Caelum and Maureen are the central characters in the novel *The Hour I First Believed* by Wally Lamb. In it, Lamb grapples with questions of faith that lie at the heart of everyday life. Among the playlist that helped him to write the novel, Lamb cites 'Losing My Religion', by US rock band R.E.M. How could a merciful deity allow Columbine to happen? Caelum's ambivalence about God turns to bitter rejection. His personal quest for meaning and faith form the human journey at the heart of this work.

The Question of Meaning

The twenty-first century has already seen protracted wars with millions of people displaced from their homes, yet another generation of children born into refugee camps, terrorism, increasing religious persecution, and devastating natural disasters in many forms. In light of this, it is difficult for people to speak of a God that is simultaneously all-powerful, just and merciful. Where is God when all of this is happening? Suffering in the world is modern atheism's weightiest argument. For many people today God does not exist.

But the quest for meaning does not fall silent. People are still seeking and searching, asking questions and looking for meaning, often in a forum other than the religious. The very fact that we engage in this quest reveals us as human beings. Walter Kasper argues that when the question of meaning is no longer asked, it implies the abdication of the person as a human being and the loss of his or her true dignity. 'Without the question about meaning and without hope, we revert back to being resourceful animals, which can find enjoyment only in material things. But then everything becomes dreary and banal.'[57] For Augustine of Hippo, writing some seventeen hundred years ago, our restlessness is the best thing about us; it stops us from settling for anything less than God. Addressing God he writes: 'You have made us for yourself alone, and our hearts are restless until they rest in thee.'

Meaning and Ultimate Meaning

The urge to ask questions is a human instinct. Questions of meaning and ultimate meaning, questions exploring the 'who' and 'why' of self, of others, of the created world and the possibility of life after death, stray across our paths from childhood. As we mature, the human instinct is to explore such questions: does my life have meaning and if so where does it come from?; do I give meaning to my own life or does my life have a meaning outside the one I give it?

The Christian world view, with its theistic foundation, naturally allows for this dimension of human life. It has within it a belief that life is ultimately meaningful, valuable and purposeful. There is more to life than what we see on the surface.

Christian Belief in God

Christians believe in the God revealed in Jesus Christ. This is the God we have met in part over the last number of chapters. However, over the years, various corrupted versions of this God have emerged, disconnected from the person of Jesus. One such image is that of the Cosmic Computer Player. This is a god who sits on high, makes judgements on his subjects and punishes at will. Like a player sitting at an enormous gaming console, this god randomly pushes buttons that can have catastrophic consequences, from the death of a child to a destructive tsunami.

A second anti-Christian image is that of the Therapeutic God whose sole function is to make us feel good about ourselves. The Therapeutic God feeds our hunger for affirmation without ever challenging destructive behaviours or helping us to discern how best to grow into the people we were made to become. Neither of these images is true to the Christian understanding of God.

The Christian God came among us as a baby, born in the humblest of circumstances. He was raised by a loving family and a mother who encouraged him and stayed with him until the moment he died, although a sword would pierce her heart. This God taught of a universal culture of love and mercy for all people and all of creation. This God suffered and died at the hands of a mob and then overcame death in the Resurrection. This God lives on in us – we are his hands and feet, his mind, heart and strength – the Body of Christ in the world today.

Further, Christians believe that relationship with God has the power to transform the human condition. We are all imperfect, incomplete. Every one of us is flawed and vulnerable. We are at our best and become our best in merciful relationships. And the most important relationship is with God.

God as Mystery

But what do we mean when we say God? For Christians, God is not one being among many, not some entity more powerful, more distant or more sympathetic than any other. God is not some invisible friend. Indeed, the word 'God' does not refer to a person at all! There is nobody out in the cosmos whose name is 'God', much older, wiser and more powerful than the average person. Theologian Michal Himes explains 'God' as a bit of shorthand which functions in Christian theology almost as the X functions in algebra. When working through an algebraic problem, one's focus is X. But X is the shorthand for the thing one doesn't know. In a similar way, God is the name of the Mystery that lies at the root of all that exists. Because we are talking about ultimate mystery we must never forget that we will never have the last word on God, never have anything close to complete comprehension. But that must not stop us trying.[58]

God as Mercy

In the Hebrew Scriptures, God's name reveals divine mercy. In the culture of the Israelites, a name was not simply a label of identification. It denoted the essence of a person. The God of the Hebrew Scriptures is utterly mysterious, indefinable; God cannot be lodged into any category of god or any human category. But in a remarkable occurrence in the Book of Exodus, God reveals God's name to Moses.

God Reveals God's Name

As the Book of Exodus opens, the situation for the people of Israel seems hopeless. They are bound in Egypt, doing the hard work of slaves. But God is a God who sees the misery of the people and hears their cries. This God answers the plight of the Israelites by enrolling Moses as their agent of deliverance. God approaches Moses at the famous episode of the burning bush.

When Moses sees the bush which seems to be burning but does not burn, he takes off his shoes, conscious that he is in the presence of something sacred. He hides his face; he does not approach. A voice calls to him, 'Moses, Moses!' (Ex 3:4). When Moses in return asks for God's name, he receives the mysterious answer: 'I am who I am.' Then God sends Moses to liberate the people.

In a dramatic movement known as 'the exodus', Moses gathers the people and leads them out of Egypt. The full revelation of God's name occurs some time later on Mount Sinai. God descends to Moses in a cloud, a sign of his mysterious presence, and discloses himself as 'God merciful and gracious' (Ex 34:6).

The message of God's mercy permeates the entire Hebrew Scriptures. Again and again God shows mercy to his errant people, despite their infidelity, in order to give them another chance for repentance and conversion. God's mercy finds special expression in the protection of the poor and the vulnerable. In contrast with the continually raised assertion that the God of the Old Testament is a jealous God of vengeance and wrath, we witness a God 'gracious and merciful, slow to anger and abounding in steadfast love' (Ex 34:6).

God as Love

Like any great religious tradition, Christianity maintains that while it cannot say everything about the Mystery that is God, it can say something. As there is no absolutely right way to talk about God, Himes uses the phrase 'least wrong way'. For Christians, the least 'wrong' way to imagine God is God as love. The New Testament repeats this over and over again in the parables and ministry of Jesus, but it is said most forthrightly in one of its very late documents, the first letter of John. In chapter four of this letter we read that God is *agape* - self-giving love (1 John 4:8,16).

The Greek word chosen to describe the love that is God is curious. The word *agape* denotes a particular kind of love. *Agape* is a purely other-directed love, one that seeks nothing in return. It is translated well as *self-gift* – the gift of oneself to another without expectation, regardless of whether the gift is accepted or rejected. The cornerstone of the Christian tradition is to bring people onto contact with the God that is self-giving love.

The Christian God is a Trinitarian God – Father, Son and Spirit – or as Augustine describes Lover, Beloved and the Love in between. So the God that is self-giving love is actually a relationship of self-giving love, between Father, Son and Spirit. Since we are created in the image of God, (not an individual person but a relationship of love), we reflect that image best when we are in loving, merciful relationships and cultivating those conditions for others.

Therefore, loving merciful relationship is the most important aspect to any Christian community. It places at its centre the invitation to personal relationship with Jesus Christ, the face of God. Children and adults alike can learn to make sense of crucial, relational experiences such as friendship, betrayal, belonging or bullying in relation to Jesus the son, the friend, the teacher, the refugee, the lost boy in the big city. Here is the God with whom all people can relate, who wants to walk the journey with each one of us, who calls us to grow into the persons of mercy we were made to be and who gives us the strength and wherewithal to do exactly that.

God in All Dimensions of Life

When C.S. Lewis was asked why he had written *The Chronicles of Narnia*, he replied that he wanted children to experience something of 'the deeper magic of life.' Through his stories, he wanted children to experience God, to encounter the power and mystery of Christ through the character of the majestic lion, Aslan. He hoped the book would help to awaken the sense of the sacred in children by engaging with real aspects of childhood. Children's sense of what is unfair, their curiosity and wonder, their dreams and disappointments – all can help to probe the mystery of God. As a Christian, C.S. Lewis believed that the presence of God pervades all dimensions of life albeit often hidden from the naked eye.

In one of the closing scenes from *The Great Gatsby*, F. Scott Fitzgerald connects the human capacity for wonder with our ability to see the mystery of God. Narrator Nick Carraway is describing the aftermath of a summer of dazzling parties Jay Gatsby's Long Island mansion:

> Most of the big shore places were closed now and there were hardly any lights except the shadowy, moving glow of a ferryboat across the Sound. And as the moon rose higher the inessential houses began to melt away until gradually I became aware

of the old island here that flowered once for Dutch sailors' eyes – a fresh, green breast of the new world. Its vanished trees, the trees that had made way for Gatsby's house, had once pandered in whispers to the last and greatest of all human dreams; for a transitory enchanted moment man must have held his breath in the presence of this continent, compelled into an aesthetic contemplation he neither understood nor desired, face to face for the last time in history with something commensurate to his capacity for wonder.[59]

Seeing beneath or behind or within what is obvious and noticing the sacred is a learned habit. Of course we can be caught unaware by something profound or beautiful and experience an unexpected connection to a life force often referred to as God. For instance, the birth of a child, a stunning view or a very moving piece of music might prompt such an experience. But rather than a 'once-off' occurrence, we can learn to notice the presence of God in the ordinary and everyday moments of our lives. It emerges from our capacity for wonder, and like any habit, it is learned with practice.

Lost in Translation

The belief that God is present in the ordinary and everyday bits and pieces of life has often been lost in time and translation. This loss is significant because of the potential effects on merciful relationship with God. The insight of theologian Richard Gaillardetz helps to make this point. In the first illustration, Figure 1, the emphasis is on the distance and difference between God and the rest of the world. In this framework, 'God is conceived as an individual being who is bigger, better, and more powerful than ourselves, but an individual nonetheless.'[60]

Figure 1[61]

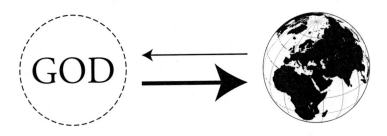

Gaillardetz believes that this is the way many Christians think about God today: God is an individual being outside the world who responds from time to time to our prayers and intercessions. If God is competing for my attention with everything else in my life, then any encounter with God will only happen at particular times, perhaps in response to prayer or participation in liturgy. In this way, life is organised in a dualistic manner between what is sacred and what is secular. So for instance, saying a prayer is sacred, while reading a novel, playing sport or doing the school run are all secular.

This understanding and image of God has many serious consequences. Primarily, if God is an individual being outside the world, then God can be confined to certain times and places, such as formal religious celebrations. If these times and places are removed, then God is removed. Rather than an abundant, overflowing mercy that 'exceeds every anticipated measure', God's mercy is constrained by time and place. This directly affects our capacity to relate to God; it is a barrier to mercy.

The second, and more authentically Christian perspective offered by Gaillardetz is radically different. In the second illustration, God is the loving and merciful ground of our existence, the very atmosphere in whom we 'live and move and have our being' (Acts 17:28). In this image, the world is in God. Within this framework, there is no such thing as a dualistic notion of what is sacred or secular. All is sacred, for all is in God; anything and everything can disclose God's mercy. This is illustrated in Figure 2.

Figure 2

From this perspective, everything in life can disclose the presence and mercy of God. When the spirit is attuned, we can notice God any time, any place – for instance at home, at work and at prayer. Those moments when we notice or experience God in our lives are referred to as sacramental moments. A sacrament is a moment of encounter with God. While we might be familiar with the seven Sacraments of the Catholic Church, we need to remember that *everything*

can disclose God's presence and so *everything* can be sacramental. But we need to learn how to see beneath or behind the obvious. To use Lewis's terms, we need to see 'the deeper magic of life'. The ability to do this is sometimes referred to as the sacramental imagination.

The sacramental imagination is key to seeing the mercy of God and therefore to merciful relationship with God. Like with any relationship, we need to notice and attend to the presence of the other. Having a sacramental imagination – the ability to notice God and God's abundant mercy in the bits and pieces of everyday – helps us into that relationship. The ability to communicate is also necessary for any relationship; and prayer is a means of communication with God. If we understand prayer as contact with God, it is perfectly natural for anyone who values that relationship to pray.

Relationship with God

We enter into relationship with that which is Mystery by learning to notice and attend to God (through sacramental imagination) and by learning to communicate with God (through prayer). While it is a natural capacity, the sacramental imagination needs to be nurtured so that it becomes part of our way of being. Habits such as the ability to pause, to be present to oneself and to become aware of the presence of others, and to notice God in our lives, cultivate the sacramental imagination. They also nurture the language of prayer.

Pope Francis encourages in particular the habit of silence. 'In order to be capable of mercy, we must dispose ourselves to listen to the Word of God.'[62] That means rediscovering the value of silence so that we can meditate on the message of God that comes to us in the everyday. Time apart to be alone, to reflect, to be silent, was essential for both John and Jesus. John's spiritual growth and development, Luke tells us, took place in the deserts (1:80).

But habits need practice. As a footballer completes thousands of drills so that a particular move becomes a natural part of his or her game, so the practice of these habits helps to develop a sacramental imagination and the language of prayer.

One real value of a sacramental imagination is the understanding of the world as sacred. Everything and every person in it is capable of revealing God's love and mercy, and is worthy of love and mercy. If we take the themes of the last four chapters we see that this is what Luke is saying: God the merciful father is revealed in Jesus Christ; we can encounter this God through our own everyday experiences: with our families, our communities – friends, colleagues, companions – and with the events and people and living creatures of the vast world we call home.

Encountering the mercy of God in this way demands a response; the only adequate response is one of mercy. We have already discussed the importance of acts of charity and sensibility of heart in rendering us capable of mercy (see Chapter Four). The third piece, the language of relationship with God, is prayer. This brings us full circle. Prayer as a means of communication with God guides us towards mercy.

The Lord's Prayer

Luke's Gospel has been called the Gospel of Prayer. It is in this Gospel, more than any other, that we hear of Jesus taking time apart to pray. This happens especially before the more important moments of his public life, such as his Baptism, the choosing of the Twelve, and in the garden before his Passion. On one particular occasion, Jesus was praying in a certain place, and when he finished, one of his disciples said to him, 'Lord, teach us to pray, as John taught his disciples' (11:1).

At the time it was customary for a Jewish rabbi to teach his followers a simple prayer they could regularly use. One of the disciples, who remains unnamed, requests something similar from Jesus. In reply, Jesus gives them what we know as the Lord's Prayer. It is not quite the form we are familiar with, which comes from Matthew's Gospel. (We know that many parts of Matthew's and Luke's Gospels come from a common source which each adapted to their own particular needs.) It is shorter and simpler but the basic structure is still the same. As such it may indeed be the earlier version and closer to what Jesus actually said.

And he said to them, 'When you pray, say:
"Father, hallowed be your name.
Your kingdom come.
Give us each day our daily bread,
and forgive us our sins,
for we ourselves forgive everyone indebted to us.
And do not bring us to the time of trial"' (11:2-4).

For centuries now Christians have been reciting the Lord's Prayer (Matthew's version) for instance before Communion at every Eucharist. As it is presented here, it is less a prayer to be recited than a group of things (petitions) around which our prayer should be centred. There are five petitions. Each one can be taken separately; each contains a theme worthy of time and reflection. When we take those themes seriously, we see that it is a very challenging prayer.

The petitions begin as follows:

Father:

We can address God as either Father or Mother; the basic meaning is that God is the source of life, that God is the Creator of every living thing. In addressing God as Father (or Mother) we are acknowledging that we are children of God. But if we are sons and daughters of the one God, then we are brothers and sisters to each other. And there can be no exceptions to this, not even one.

When we pray to God as 'Father' we are saying that we see every single person on the face of the earth, irrespective of race, nationality, skin colour, class, occupation, age or religion as our brothers and sisters. If not, we have to stop praying at this first word.

Hallowed be your name:

For the Jews, a name was not simply an identifying label. It denoted the whole person. In this petition we are praying that God's self and not just God's name be revered by all. God's holiness (ie merciful goodness, differing in kind to human goodness) in no way depends on us. God's name is already holy; we need to hold it that way in our hearts. Even the tone of voice we use when we utter a person's name communicates how we feel about them. In this petition we are asking that the whole world recognise the holiness of God. God does not need this but we do; when we say this in all sincerity then we are saying that we belong to God and recognise God in our lives.

What we are asking is that God's holiness be acknowledged not only by our words but by the way we live. In other words, it is a prayer that God's holiness be reflected in our own lives and in the lives of every person. It is, in fact, another way of expressing the following petition …

Your kingdom come:
God's kingdom, as we have already noted, is a universal culture where God's mercy and love prevails, rather than any human measure. In that kingdom, God's mercy and love abounds in people's hearts and minds and relationships. When people live in that kingdom they experience the love and mercy of God, in themselves and in the way they interact with others. It produces a world of freedom and joy, of peace and justice for all.

In praying this petition we are not simply asking God to create this culture while we sit back and wait. We are also committing ourselves to be partners with God in making it happen. Our co-operation in this work is of vital importance. Christians believe that to be a disciple of Jesus it is essential to be involved in the task of making this universal culture of mercy a reality. And it has to begin right now; it is not to be left in total to a future existence. The kingdom of God is not only a future reality. This apparently simple phrase is a prayer that through our involvement, God's kingdom will come to pass. It is taxing to its core.

Give us each day our daily bread:

We pray that we will be always provided with what we need for daily living. But that 'us' is universal. If my prayer is confined to my family, my friends, my colleagues and companions, even my village, town or city, it misses the point. The 'us' refers to all God's children without exception. We are praying that every single person be supplied with their daily needs.

But that cannot happen unless we all get involved. This petition does not simply leave the concern at God's door. The feeding of all the world's people is the responsibility of all the people of the world. Yet millions are hungry. Countless numbers suffer from malnutrition as well as being deprived of many of the other essentials of dignified living. 16 per cent of the Irish population lives on an income which is less than the official poverty line – about €210 per adult per week. Given a population of approximately 4.58 million people this implies that almost 730,000 live at risk of poverty.[63] One in six Americans lives in a household that is 'food insecure', meaning that in any given month, they will be out of money, out of food, and forced to miss meals or seek assistance to feed themselves. Nationally, more than fifty million Americans are food insecure. Among the hungry are nearly seventeen million children.[64]

This petition extends to those who live in spiritual hunger, such as those who suffer depression. Major depression is a period of overwhelming sadness. It involves a loss of interest in activity, even those activities that used to bring pleasure. Those feelings are usually accompanied by other emotional and physical symptoms. Postnatal (postpartum) depression is an example of this.

Many new mothers go through the baby blues. This 'feeling down' is caused by hormonal changes following childbirth, by lack of sleep, and by everything that goes with taking care of a new baby. Symptoms include mood swings, sadness, feeling unable to cope and fatigue. These feelings usually pass within a week or two. However, in some cases, it develops into postnatal (postpartum) depression, where these feelings drag on and escalate, and the new mother feels unable to cope and just wants to withdraw. Fortunately, most people can be treated effectively.[65]

Spiritual and material hungers are part of our universal concern when we pray that all of 'us' have 'our' daily bread. Again, the challenge of the prayer is plain. It is even more pronounced when we say it in the Eucharist. The Eucharist is the sacrament or sign of a merciful community that takes care of all its members, especially those in need. If we leave the Eucharistic table and ignore this responsibility then our participation has been little more than a charade.

Forgive us our sins, for we ourselves forgive everyone indebted to us:
Here we pray in repentance for the wrongs we have committed and past behaviour that is less than our best. But it is conditional, linking us once again to all those around us. We pray that God will forgive us all that we have done wrong, just as we have forgiven all those who

we feel have done wrong to us. This petition throws us dramatically back on ourselves. We are praying to share God's own readiness to forgive that is emblematic of his infinite mercy.

How easily we say this again and again when we recite the Our Father. But we cannot really understand God's forgiveness without the experience of forgiving and the forgiveness of others. Pope Francis insists that God asks us, above all, not to judge and not to condemn. 'If anyone wishes to avoid God's judgment, he should not make himself the judge of his brother or sister. Human beings, whenever they judge, look no further than the surface, whereas the Father looks into the very depths of the soul.'[66] We all know that at times forgiveness and reconciliation can be very difficult. Yet it must be part and parcel of Christian living; God is so ready to forgive. Our deepest urge should be to rehabilitate and restore to life rather than condemn and punish.

Do not bring us to the time of trial:
We are surrounded by forces which can draw us away from God and all that is best in ourselves and our world. This petition asks that we will not succumb permanently to such negative energies. We constantly need God's helping hand to lift us up. This is the one petition where we depend totally on God's help. We are asking God to protect us from the trials that could befall us and that have befallen others. 'Do not put us to the test.'

This petition acknowledges that life is not easy. In fact it is full of influences that harden our hearts: influences that persuade us that we need more, that tempt us into blind consumerism, that lull us into becoming bystanders. This allows society to turn a blind eye to the desperate needs of others. There is also the temptation to consider ourselves self-sufficient and needless of God. We have encountered the reality of these trials and more in previous chapters. Against all of these God is calling us. God is always turned towards us, ready to come to our assistance. 'The assistance we ask for is already the first step of God's mercy towards us ... Day after day, touched by his compassion, we also can become compassionate towards others.'[67] We pray here that God will enable us to deal with the things that harden our hearts and prevent that sensibility that allows us to be merciful.

The Disciples and Prayer

It is worth noting that up to this point in his account, Luke's emphasis is on the prayer life of Jesus. The disciples are not generally characterised as men of prayer in the Gospels. Jesus' prayer life was, even in the garden of Gethsemane, something which he practised alone.

But an unnamed disciple who has noticed his practice as a pattern, asks him to teach the disciples to pray. This request was an open admission that they felt that without prayer their lives were deficient. In the Book of Acts which is also attributed to Luke, the prayer life which characterises Jesus will characterise the disciples as well. Here Luke is paving the way, laying the foundation for the communion with God in prayer that will galvanise and cement the early Christian community.

It is interesting that the subject of prayer is raised by one of the disciples, rather than by Jesus. For

Jesus, prayer was vital. But as strongly as he believed in prayer and practised it personally, he did not initiate the subject. It is likely that Jesus wanted the disciples to conclude on their own how important prayer is. Jesus is ready and willing to teach on prayer, but only when his disciples are eager to learn.

It is no accident that the disciple asks Jesus to teach them to pray at the very time that Jesus is himself at prayer. They had witnessed the effects of prayer on Jesus - how it strengthened, enlivened and consoled him. It was enough eventually for them to want to engage in prayer themselves. Their desire is clear. But prayer does not come easy. They need words, they need a method, they need advice. That is true of many people today. The habit of prayer does not come easy. There are very many forms of prayer and ways of praying. Different approaches suit different people. It is often a question of trial and error – and perseverance.

While the Lord's Prayer is beautiful it is also challenging. Much more than a prayer of petition, it is also a statement of who we are and 'whose' we are. We belong to God and to each other. The 'most perfect of prayers,' it is a plan of hope for living with a heart of mercy. We affirm our divine potential every time we pray it.

We Belong to God and to Each Other
In Stef Penney's award-winning novel *The Tenderness of Wolves*, the trapper Parker tells Mrs Ross of an abandoned wolf cub he once found and brought up as a dog. That is, until:

It remembered it was a wolf, not a pet. It stared into the distance. Then one day it was gone. The Chippewa have a word for it – it means 'the sickness of long thinking'. You cannot tame a wild animal, because it will always remember where it is from, and yearn to go back.[68]

There is something at the heart of every living thing that remembers where it is from and yearns to go back. At some unfathomable depth there is a pull, a tug, reminding us of who we really are. Remember that moment when the prodigal son has hit rock bottom, alone in a foreign land, he 'comes to himself' (15.17). In that dawning realisation the younger son understands who he really is, where he is from, and yearns to go back.

The 'sickness of long thinking' is prevalent today, typified by the loneliness among young people and the spiritual hunger widespread in Western culture that I addressed in Chapter One. Only by acknowledging who and whose we are can healing of this sickness take place. We belong to God and to each other. Discovering who and whose we are, lies at the heart of a merciful relationship with God.

The story of the prodigal son (or the merciful father) in Chapter Two highlights the potential of relationship with God. Just as the father acts, so too does the Father act. The relationship of mercy is based on human dignity – the dignity that God has bestowed and is proper to every person. Divine mercy leads human beings to a return to the truth about themselves.

Mercy Begets Mercy

The experience of mercy enables us to be merciful. In the final paragraphs of *Oliver Twist*, Charles Dickens explicitly expresses the rippling effects of God's merciful care:

> how the two orphans [Oliver and Rose], tried by adversity, remembered its lessons in mercy to others, and mutual love and fervent thanks to Him who had protected and preserved them – these are all the matters which need not be told. I have said that they were truly happy; and without strong affection, and humanity of heart, and gratitude to that Being whose code is Mercy, and whose great attribute is Benevolence to all things that breathe, true happiness can never be attained.[69]

True happiness depends on faithfulness between individuals that results in human kindness; sensibility of heart especially for those in need; relationship with God whose code is mercy.

Harden Not Our Hearts

Today's excited society keeps us busy with trivia, our heads full of noise, incapable of pausing to hear the cries of others. Our culture can descend into apathy and indifference, potentially blocking the wellsprings of mercy. It can be tempted to close in on itself, to confine living to private life, to be suspicious of strangers and unmoved by the stories of others. But on the other hand the witness of real mercy touches people profoundly.

This is key to the 'Francis effect' – the impact the pope has had on the world at large. His words about mercy are strong; his merciful gestures even stronger.

This is also true of ordinary people. Our capacity for mercy is huge, often most obvious when tragedy strikes and people come together in compassion and care. We have seen this again and again in this country, for instance in the reaction of the people of Galway to the horrific murder of Swiss student Manuela Riedo.

In October 2007, seventeen-year-old Swiss student Manuela was murdered at an isolated spot in Galway just two days after she arrived in Ireland to study English. The reaction of Galwegians was sincere and immediate, including a foundation set up in Manuela's memory to help her parents cope and allow them return to the city each year to mark their daughter's anniversary.

Mrs Riedo has commented that the foundation and the work it does, as well as the friendships she and her husband have formed in Ireland, is what gives them comfort. She speaks also of her gratitude that Manuela's memory continues to burn so strongly in the hearts of the people of Galway.

Mercy – faithfulness between individuals that results in human kindness.

Mercy – sensibility of heart for those in need.

When the merciful heart of humanity beats strong, it reveals something of the divine mercy within us. This is what the sickness of long thinking reveals. The capacity for wonder, the search for meaning, the propensity for mercy – these are all expressions of the divine spark within.

Experiences of Mercy Point to God

During the exodus, Moses increasingly wants to see the face of God. But God answers Moses, 'I will show mercy. But … you cannot see my face' (Exodus 33:20).

Moses cannot see God just as we cannot see God. But we can identify God by his mercy. We can recognise the mercy of God by reflecting on human experience, on Scripture and on our own lives. In and through history, today as much as any day, God reveals his essence if we have eyes to see. God's mystery is disclosed in his mercy. Mercy is the expression of his divine essence.

If mercy is God's own attribute, if God's name reveals divine mercy, then our encounters with mercy can be seen as pointers to the very existence of God. Sebastian Barry, in his play *The Steward of Christendom*, conveys this well.

Knowing that his father will 'put down' the family dog that has killed a sheep, the little boy stays out all night with the dog. He returns at dawn to meet his father:

Down at last into the yard we came, the dog skulking on the rope just the same as the day he had arrived to us, and my father came out from the house in his big clothes. All brown with clothes and hair. It was as if I had never seen him before, never looked in his entirety, from head to toe, and I knew then that the dog and me were for slaughter. My feet carried me on to where he stood, immortal you would say in the door. And he pulled me to him so that my cheek rested against the buckle of his belt. And he raised his own face to the brightening sky and praised someone, in a crushed voice, God maybe, for my safety and stroked my hair. And the dog's crime was never spoken of, but that he lived till he died. And I would call that the mercy of fathers, when the love that lies in them deeply like the glittering face of a well is betrayed by an emergency, and the child sees at last that he is loved, loved and needed and not to be lived without, and greatly.[70]

The gift of mercy allows the father to see into the child and into his own heart; to see further than the folly, the misbehaviour or the guilty dog. It is without words, beyond words. Love begets love, mercy begets mercy. 'What a beautiful truth of faith this is for our lives: the mercy of God! God's love for us is so great, so deep; it is an unfailing love, one which always takes us by the hand and supports us, lifts us up and leads us on.'[71]

Endnotes

1. See Walter Kasper. *Mercy: The Essence of the Gospel and the Key to Christian Life*, trans. W. Madges (New York: Paulist Press, 2014), 43.
2. See Kasper, 11, 21.
3. Charles Dickens. *Oliver Twist*, (Hertfordshire: Wordsworth Editions, 2000), 120.
4. William Shakespeare. *The Merchant of Venice*. Act IV Scene 1
5. Pope Francis, *Misericordiae Vultus*. (Dublin: Veritas, 2015).
6. *Misericordiae Vultus*.
7. *Misericordiae Vultus*.
8. See for instance Howard Chua-Eoan and Elizabeth Dias, *Pope Francis, The People's Pope* http://poy.time.com/2013/12/11/person-of-the-year-pope-francis-the-peoples-pope/ (accessed 26 September 2015).
9. See Kasper, 112.
10. See Kasper, translator's preface, xii-xiii.
11. Kasper, 43-44.
12. Muall Selcuk. 'Opening the Eye of the Heart.' *Religious Education* volume 110, no.3 (May-June 2015).
13. PovertyUSA is the domestic anti-poverty program of the U.S. Catholic Bishops. An initiative of the Catholic Campaign for Human Development (CCHD), PovertyUSA seeks to educate and promote understanding about poverty and its root causes. See www.povertyusa.org.
14. Kasper, 40.
15. *Misericordiae Vultus*.
16. *Misericordiae Vultus*.
17. *Misericordiae Vultus*.
18. Ibid.
19. Pope Francis. *Evangelii Gaudium* (Dublin: Veritas, 2013), 273, 133-134.
20. Black, Grant, cited in Gil, Natalie. Loneliness: a silent plague that is hurting young people most. The *Guardian*, 20 July 2014.
21. Kross, Ethan et al. (2013) Facebook Use Predicts Declines in Subjective Well-Being in Young Adults. http://journals.plos.org/plosone/article?id=10.1371/journal.pone.0069841 (accessed April 10th 2015)
22. Sutherland, Ruth, cited in Gil, 2014.
23. Charles Dickens. *Oliver Twist*, 266.
24. Chapman, Mike. 'Adding Up the Oprah Effect The Book Club sold over 20 million branded editions.' http://www.adweek.com/news/television/adding-oprah-effect-132140 (accessed April 10th 2015).
25. Tolle, Eckhart. *A New Earth: Awakening to Your Life's Purpose* (Penguin Group, 2005), 6–7.

26. Wiesel, Eli. Cited in Barnes & Noble Editorial Reviews http://www.barnesandnoble.com/w/night-elie-wiesel/1116731697?ean=9780374500016 (accessed 10 April 2015).

27. Pope Francis. *Evangelii Gaudium* (Dublin: Veritas, 2013), 2.

28. *Misericordiae Vultus.*

29. May Sarton. 'Now I Become Myself,' *Collected Poems, 1930–1973*, (New York: Norton, 1974), 156

30. From Brian Doyle. *Leaping: Revelations and Epiphanies* (Chicago: Loyola Press, 2013,) 180-181. We used this quote in *Credo* Book 6, p. 155.

31. Charles Dickens, *Oliver Twist*, 51-52.

32. *Misericordiae Vultus*, 14.

33. We used this story in *Living and Loving as Disciples of Christ, Credo* Book 6, chapter 9.

34. Kasper, 210.

35. http://oblatesosbbelmont.org/traditional-marian-prayers/ For the original translation see Kasper, 212.

36. See for example Stella O'Malley. *Cotton Wool Kids: What's Making Irish Parents Paranoid?* (Cork: Mercier Press, 2015).

37. Kahlil Gibran. 'On Children,' http://www.goodreads.com/author/quotes/6466154.Kahlil_Gibran (accessed 26 September 2015).

38. F. Scott Fitzgerald, *The Great Gatsby*, http://genius.com/F-scott-fitzgerald-the-great-gatsby-chapter-ix-annotated/ (accessed July 20th 2015).

39. Pope Francis, *Strengthen Your Hearts*. http://www.romereports.com/2015/01/27/read-pope-francis-full-lenten-message (accessed 14th July 2015).

40. Taken from *Son of God Son of Mary, Credo* book 2, 202-203.

41. Chapter Statement of the Congregation of the Sisters of Mercy http://www.sistersofmercy.ie/vision/index.cfm (accessed September 26th 2015).

42. Claudia Croft, 'Mind What You Buy', in *The Sunday Times Style*, 7 June 2015, p.33

43. Pope Francis. *Evangelii Gaudium*, n.54.

44. Susan Abulhawa. *Mornings in Jenin*, (New York: Bloomsbury, 2010), 3.

45. Robert Fisk, cited in Susan Abulhawa. *Mornings in Jenin*, Chapter 33.

46. Stephen Mitchell (ed). 'Ah, Not to Be Cut Off', in *Ahead of All Parting: The Selected Poems and Prose of Rainer Maria Rilke* (New York: Modern Library, 1995), 191.

47. Fr Peter McVerry. Homily on the Feast of St Ignatius of Loyola – 31 July 2015. See http://www.gardinerstparish.ie/news (accessed 2 August 2015).

48. Dietrich von Hildebrand & John Henry Crosby, *My Battle Against Hitler: Faith, Truth, and Defiance in the Shadow of the Third Reich* (Colorado: Image, 2014).

49. Harper Lee, *To Kill A Mockingbird* (J. B. Lippincott Company: Philadelphia & New York, 1960), 195.

50. Juliet Macur, *Cycle of Lies: The Fall of Lance Armstrong* (London: William Collins, 2014), 196

51. Welcoming the Stranger: Affirmations for Faith Leaders UNHCR http://www.unhcr.org/51b6de419.html

52. For his full homily see http://www.news.va/en/news/pope-on-lampedusa-the-globalization-of-indifferenc (accessed 13 July 2015).

53. See http://mobile.nytimes.com/2015/09/04/world/europe/syria-boy-drowning.html?_r=1&referrer= (and http://www.independent.co.uk/news/world/europe/aylan-kurdis-story-how-a-small-syrian-child-came-to-be-washed-up-on-a-beach-in-turkey-10484588.html (accessed 29 September 2015).

54. Austen Iveteigh. '*Laudato Si*': A landmark in modern church teaching that will shape a new future, http://cvcomment.org/2015/06/17/laudato-si-a-landmark-in-modern-church-teaching-that-will-shape-a-new-future/ (accessed 26 September 2015).

55. Charles Dickens, *Oliver Twist*, 207.

56. Albert Einstein, quoted by http://www.goodreads.com/quotes/369-a-human-being-is-a-part-of-the-whole-called (accessed 30 September 2015).

57. Kasper, 3.

58. Michael J. Himes & McNeill, D. P., *Doing the Truth in Love: Conversations about God, Relationships, and Service* (New York: Paulist Press, 1995), Chapter 1.

59. F. Scott Fitzgerald, *The Great Gatsby*, http://genius.com/F-scott-fitzgerald-the-great-gatsby-chapter-ix-annotated/ (accessed 26 September 2015).

60. Richard R. Gaillardetz. *Transforming Our Days: Spirituality, Community, and Liturgy in a Technological Culture* (New York: Crossroad, 2000), 47.

61. These images are copied from Ibid., 48-50.

62. *Misericordiae Vultus*.

63. http://www.nerinstitute.net/blog/2013/05/08/working-and-living-below-the-poverty-line-the-work/ (accessed 20 July 2015).

64. U.S. Dept. of Agriculture, 2012, cited by http://www.worldvisionusprograms.org/us_poverty_myths.php (accessed 20 July 2015).

65. According to the US National Institute of Mental Health (NIMH), about 10 to 15 per cent of women develop postpartum depression. See http://www.nimh.nih.gov/health/publications/depression/index.shtml and http://www.healthline.com/health/depression/facts-statistics-infographic#1 (accessed 26 September 2015).

66. *Misericordiae Vultus*.

67. *Misericordiae Vultus*.

68. Stef Penney. *The Tenderness of Wolves* (London, Hachette UK, 2007), 154.

69. Charles Dickens, *Oliver Twist*, 360.

70. Sebastian Barry, *The Steward of Christendom*. We used this quote in *Credo* Book 6, Chapter 7, 155.

71. Homily of Pope Francis: Papal mass for the possession of the chair of the Bishop of Rome. Divine Mercy Sunday, 7 April 2013 https://w2.vatican.va/content/francesco/en/homilies/2013/documents/papa-francesco_20130407_omelia-possesso-cattedra-laterano.html (accessed 21 July 2015).